# Lector's Guide to
# Biblical
# Pronunciations,
# Updated

# Lector's Guide to
# Biblical
# Pronunciations,
# Updated

## Joseph M. Staudacher

**Professor Emeritus of Speech**
**Marquette University**

Our Sunday Visitor Publishing Division
Our Sunday Visitor, Inc.
Huntington, Indiana 46750

Dedicated to
my children and their spouses:

*Lynn Mary*
*Michael Joseph*
*Jane Mary and George*
*Ann Mary and Steven*
*Joan Mary and Michael*
*Rosemary and Dale,*

whose names enunciate the
power of the Lord.

———————

# Acknowledgments

I wish to thank those who gave special help: Professor Alfred J. Sokolnicki, former Dean of the College of Speech, Marquette University, who proposed the original idea for this guide; and to Father Thomas Caldwell, S.J., of the Marquette University Theology Department, who steered me to the right sources and was ever helpful whenever the need arose and to my late wife, Rose, who typed the final manuscript.

I am grateful to Westminster Press, Philadelphia, Pennsylvania, whose *New Westminster Dictionary of the Bible*, edited by Henry Snyder Gehman and published in 1970, was one of the primary sources that motivated me to come up with this guide.

I also wish to thank Edward Huff, a student at Saint Meinrad Seminary in Indiana, for his research on this updated version of this guide.

# Contents

# Introduction to
## Updated Edition 2001

No one could have envisioned how popular this little book would be at the time of its original publication in 1975. Since then, Professor Staudacher's work has been a mainstay in almost every sacristy, ambo, and new lector's pocket throughout the English-speaking world.

The current revision and updated version was deemed necessary in light of a new translation of the Roman Lectionary that was approved for use starting on the First Sunday of Advent 1998. Over one hundred words have been added to this new edition and a new format has been added while at the same time retaining the original rendering with some minor corrections.

This current edition gives the lector two ways to look up words for each Sunday's readings: either by turning to the Sunday of the Year in question and there encountering words that the author has determined may pose a problem for some or by turning to the alphabetized list in the back for a more comprehensive listing. We feel this new option will ensure the continued usefulness of this little aid to the effective proclamation of God's Word.

MICHAEL DUBRUIEL
ACQUISITIONS EDITOR
OUR SUNDAY VISITOR

# Introduction
## to Original Edition

The author examined carefully the eleven hundred or more pages of the Roman Lectionary, a volume containing scriptural passages for all the Masses in the new three-year cycle, for words which might cause the public reader difficulty in pronunciation: persons, places, and things.

Three possibilities for designating acceptable pronunciation were open to use: diacritical markings as found in most dictionaries, phonetics, and respelling.

For reasons explained later in these pages, respelling was selected as the easiest method of making pronunciations clear. It is hoped that the public reader will find the method helpful.

J.M.S.

# The Purpose of This Manual

The purpose of this manual is to help those who read the Scriptures aloud in the liturgy to do so efficiently and acceptably, particularly with regard to the difficult pronunciations of persons, places, and things found in readings assigned for the three-year cycle.

Before examining pronunciation in principle and practice, a review of the broader structure of scriptural proclamation in terms of general and basic principles is presented:

1. Public readers of Scripture are messengers of the Word of God.
2. Public readers of Scripture become better messengers by better understanding their message.
3. Public readers of Scripture become better messengers through rehearsal and performance.

4. Public readers of Scripture become better messengers by developing skills in visual and vocal technique.

   a. Visual technique is revealed through bodily response. Bodily response in this case is not open, broad gesture but rather, *subtle* bodily expression and muscle tone.

   b. Vocal technique is revealed through sufficient volume and projection, a conversational melody-pattern, variety in tone-color, the use of pace and pause, crisp enunciation, and finally acceptable pronunciation.

# The Problem

Our alphabet has twenty-six letters to express as many as thirty-nine sounds. Our alphabet, therefore, is incomplete. Sometimes the same letter has to play several roles. For example, the letter "A" is used to express six different sounds: PLATE, CAROL, PAT, FATHER, ALL, and SOFA.

Strictly speaking, our alphabet does not have twenty-six separate letters. C is either S or K; Q is K; and X is KS. Therefore our alphabet has only twenty-three letters to express as many as thirty-nine sounds.

A second disadvantage in our limited alphabet is found in the pronunciation of some letter combinations. One example among many is the letter combination OUGH. These letters are pronounced differently in the words THOUGH, ROUGH, THROUGH, and COUGH.

To solve the problem of the inconsistency in pronouncing these and other letter combinations, three systems are possible: phonetics, diacritical markings, and respelling.

Phonetics, a system that uses a separate symbol for each vowel and consonant sound, was established by a group of international scholars in 1888. The same symbol always stands for the same sound, and the same sound is always represented by the same symbol whether the language be English, German, French, or any other. As a result, phonetics may be considered the most accurate way of representing vowel and consonant sounds for accurate pronunciation. The only difficulty is the fact that the system of phonetics is not generally taught in our schools, as are reading, writing, and arithmetic, and as a result, few persons are able to read phonetics.

A second method of indicating speech sounds with visual symbols is the system of diacritical markings found in dictionaries. These markings are helpful, but unfortunately they differ in part from one dictionary to another. This lack of consistency can be confusing.

A third method is respelling, a system that this pronunciation guide follows. An attempt is made to spell the words in such a way that the acceptable pronunciation is immediately clear and obvious. For example, Deuteronomy is listed as Dyoo-ter-AH-nuh-mee.

To standardize the sounds of the words that will be visualized, the following *pronunciation key* is offered. Two basic assumptions underlie the use of the key in its application to the pronunciation of biblical terms:

1. No sounds foreign to American speech are introduced: for example, no rolled *r* or German or Scottish *ch* in ich or loch.
2. The pronunciations are based on General American. Those who speak with Eastern or Southern speech are encouraged to make their own adjustments wherever needed.
   In the pronunciation key that follows, notice that **OO** is a short vowel sound as in B**OO**K while the plain OO is a long vowel sound as in MOON. Notice, too, that the **TH** sound is the voiced **TH** as in **TH**EE while the plain TH is the breath TH sound as in THREE. Finally, notice that the accented syllable is in capital letters as in UHN-der-laind (underlined).

# A Key to Pronouncing
# Words in Respelling

## VOWEL SOUNDS

EE as in eat, beet, shriek
&#10038; EET, BEET, SHREEK

IH as in bit, myth, build
&#10038; BIHT, MIHTH, BIHLD

AY as in ace, aid, deign
&#10038; AYS, AYD, DAYN

EH as in ebb, wreck, bread
&#10038; EHB, WREHK, BREHD

A as in pat, slab, map
&#10038; PAT, SLAB, MAP

AH as in farmer, car, heart
&#10038; FAHR-mer, KAHR, HAHRT

AW as in law, taught, appall
&#10038; LAW, TAWT, uh-PAWL

O as in home, coat, abode
&#10038; HOM, KOT, uh-BOD

**OO** as in book, bull, woman
> BOOK, BOOL, WOO-m'n

OO as in moon, food, do
> MOON, FOOD, DOO

UH as in cut, love, nut
> KUHT, LUHV, NUHT

ER as in bird, hurt, earn
> BERD, HERT, ERN

EHR as in air, fare, square
> EHR, FEHR, SKWEHR

AI as in ice, fly, bide
> AIS, FLAI, BAID

AU as in out, how, down
> AUT, HAU, DAUN

OI as in boy, coin, voice
> BOI, KOIN, VOIS

## Consonant Sounds

P as in push, oppose, nap
> POOSH, uh-POZ, NAP

B as in better, rub, blubber
> BEH-ter, RUHB, BLUH-ber

T as in tin, bit, letter
➤ TIHN, BIHT, LEHTER

D as in dome, bad, redder
➤ DOM, BAD, REH-der

K as in king, link, lucky
➤ KIHNG, LIHNGK, LUH-kee

G as in gun, lug, nugget
➤ GUHN, LUHG, NUH-guht

F as in from, leaf, muffle
➤ FRUHM, LEEF, MUH-f'l

V as in vine, move, lover
➤ VAIN, MOOV, LUH-ver

TH as in thin, myth, zither
➤ THIHN, MIHTH, ZIH-ther

***TH*** as in then, this, mother
➤ ***TH***EHN, ***TH***IHS, MUH-*th*er

S as in sum, pace, lesser
➤ SUHM, PAYS, LEH-ser

Z as in zoo, topaz, easy
➤ ZOO, TO-paz, EE-zee

SH as in sure, hush, gusher
➤ SHOOR, HUHSH, GUH-sher

ZH as in azure, garage, mirage
	➻ AZH-*oo*r, guh-RAHZH, mih-RAHZH

H as in hat, ahead, who
	➻ HAT, uh-HEHD, HOO

M as in man, name, mummy
	➻ MAN, NAYM, MUH-mee

N as in not, ran, sinner
	➻ NAHT, RAN, SIH-ner

NG as in sing, running, bank
	➻ SIHNG, RUHN-ihng, BANGK

W as in win, one, weather
	➻ WIHN, WUHN, WEH-*th*er

L as in leap, pool, allow
	➻ LEEP, POOL, uh-LAU

R as in run, car, arrow
	➻ RUHN, KAHR, EHR-o

Y as in you, onion, canyon
	➻ YOO, UHN-yuhn, KAN-yuhn

TSH as in church, chance, chipper
	➻ TSHERTSH, TSHANS, TSHIH-per

DZH as in Jim, John, edge
	➻ DZHIHM, DZHAHN, EHDZH

# Definition *

Pronunciation is the expression of sounds and accents of words in connected speech and in conformity with acceptable standards. From this definition of pronunciation four key elements arise: sounds, accents, connected speech, and acceptable standards.

a. *Sounds.* The basic ingredients of spoken words are vowel and consonant sounds. Mispronunciations occur when vowel or consonant sounds are added, omitted, or substituted.

Words can be mispronounced when sounds are added or changed:

|  | *Wrong* | *Correct* |
|---|---|---|
| Arthritis | ahr-ther-AI-tihs | ahr-THRAI-tihs |
| Chicago | tshih-CAW-go | shih-CAW-go |
|  |  | (also shih-CAH-go) |
| Athletics | ath-uh-LEH-tihks | ath-LEH-tihks |

---

* See *Laymen, Proclaim the Word,* Joseph M. Staudacher, Franciscan Herald Press, Chicago, 1973, pages 47-49.

22

Words can be mispronounced when sounds are omitted:

|  | *Wrong* | *Correct* |
|---|---|---|
| Aluminum | uh-LOOM-nuhm | uh-LOOM-ih-nuhm |
| Library | LAI-behr-ee | LAI-brehr-ee |
| Honorable | AH-ner-b**oo**l | AH-ner-uh-b**oo**l |

Words can be mispronounced when sounds are substituted:

|  | *Wrong* | *Correct* |
|---|---|---|
| February | FEHB-yoo-ehr-ee | FEHB-roo-ehr-ee |
| Them | dehm | *th*ehm |
| Until | ahn-TIHL | uhn-TIHL |

b. *Accents.* Accents, as used here, do not refer to foreign accent but to the stress placed on a syllable of a word. Some words admit of differently accented syllables. Some words do not. A word can be mispronounced, therefore, by misplacing the accent.

|  | *Wrong* | *Correct* |
|---|---|---|
| Museum | MYOO-zee-oom | myoo-ZEE-oom |

| Detroit | DEE-troit | dee-TROIT |
| Theater | thee-AY-ter | THEE-uh-ter |

c. *Connected speech*. Connected speech refers to the pronunciation of words, not as single words, but as used in combination with other words. For example, the word BECAUSE is usually pronounced bee-KAWZ as an individual word, but in connected speech, unless the speaker wishes to emphasize BECAUSE, he may acceptably pronounce it bee-KUHZ. The purpose of speech is communication, and not to call undue attention to itself. Readers who pronounce every syllable of every word in connected speech the way they pronounce words singly, fail to follow Shakespeare's wise advice:

*"Speak the speech, I pray you, as I pronounced it to you, trippingly on the tongue, but if you mouth it as many of your players do, I had as lief the town crier spoke my lines."*

Connected speech permits no pauses in the sentence "Pat takes science." Pausing after "Pat" or "takes" would be affected and overdone.

Examples of other pronunciation variations in connected speech involve the simple words A (UH) and THE (*TH*UH).

Don't say AY MAN. Say UH MAN. Use AY only for emphasis. For example, "I didn't ask all of you to help. I asked for AY (one) helper."

Don't say *TH*EE MAN. Say *TH*UH MAN or better *TH'* MAN. Say *TH*EE for emphasis. For example, "He is *TH*EE man of the hour." Or say *TH*EE before a vowel sound. For example, *TH*EE APPLE or *TH*EE F.H.A. Even though *F* in F.H.A. is called a consonant, it begins with a vowel sound.

    d. *Acceptable standards.* An acceptable standard is a model agreed upon by experts for imitation. There is no one pronunciation standard that is acceptable for all words in the English language. Variations are easily discernible in the speech of cultured British, Canadian, Australian, and American persons. In the speech of cultured Americans we find three general classifications: Eastern, Southern, and General American, and even in these classifications we recognize acceptable variations.

While it may be emotionally difficult for some persons to be tolerant of pronunciations of different areas, it must be admitted that language is the result of usage and not of preconceived rules. This is not to say that because thousands of persons say *toity-toid* for *thirty-third* or *dis* for *this* or *hep* for *help*, that these pronunciations are correct. Each locality has its unacceptable provincialisms. What we are looking for is a more general acceptability and uniformity. Since this uniformity is found more frequently among the better educated users of language, we look to them for our model of imitation. The principle of pronunciation which we derive from the foregoing reasoning is this: *Pronounce words the way the majority of better-educated persons in your general area pronounce them.*

To determine what pronunciations are used by the better educated persons in your area, listen to radio and television announcers on reputable stations as well as public speakers, teachers, and others well versed in language. Choose those pronunciations for your own that sound most general and least different.

Finally, with regard to the pronunciation of biblical names, places, and things, listen to rabbis, pastors, and priests. They have had a broad religious background and specific training in Scripture.

The pronunciations used in this guide are traditionally and generally accepted by those who proclaim the Scriptures as public readers in the Church.

# Words by Each Sunday in the Three-Year Cycle

## YEAR A

### Season of Advent

**FIRST SUNDAY OF ADVENT**

*First Reading*

| | |
|---|---|
| Isaiah | ai-ZAY-uh |
| Amoz | AY-muhz |
| Judah | DZHOO-duh |
| Jerusalem | dzheh-ROO-suh-lehm |
| Zion | ZAI-uhn |

*Gospel*

| | |
|---|---|
| Noah | NO-uh |

**SECOND SUNDAY OF ADVENT**

*First Reading*

| | |
|---|---|
| Jesse | DZHEH-see |
| Gentiles | DZHEHN-tailz |

*Gospel*

| | |
|---|---|
| Judea | dzhoo-DEE-uh |
| Pharisees | FEHR-ih-seez |
| Sadducees | SAD-dzhoo-seez |

## THIRD SUNDAY OF ADVENT
*First Reading*

| | |
|---|---|
| Lebanon | LEH-buh-nuhn |
| Carmel | KAHR-muhl |
| Sharon | SHEHR-uhn |
| Zion | ZAI-uhn |

## FOURTH SUNDAY OF ADVENT
*First Reading*

| | |
|---|---|
| Ahaz | AY-haz |
| Isaiah | ai-ZAY-uh |
| Emmanuel | eh-MAN-yoo-ehl |

*Second Reading*

| | |
|---|---|
| Gentiles | DZHEHN-tailz |

*Gospel*

| | |
|---|---|
| Betrothed | bee-TRO*TH*D |
| Emmanuel | eh-MAN-yoo-ehl |

# YEAR A

## Season of Christmas

### Christmas — Vigil Mass

*First Reading*

| | |
|---|---|
| Zion | ZAI-uhn |
| Jerusalem | dzheh-ROO-suh-lehm |
| Vindication | vihn-dih-KAY-shuhn |
| Diadem | DAI-uh-dehm |
| Espoused | eh-SPAUZD |

*Second Reading*

| | |
|---|---|
| Antioch | AN-tih-ahk |
| Pisidia | pih-SIH-dih-uh |
| Synagogue | SIHN-uh-gahg |
| Israelites | IHZ-rih-ehl-aits |
| Israel | IHZ-ray-ehl |
| Sojourn | SO-dzhern |
| Jesse | DZHEH-see |

*Gospel*

| | |
|---|---|
| Genealogy | dzhee-nee-AH-lo-dzhee |
| Abraham | AY-bruh-ham |
| Isaac | AI-zuhk |
| Jacob | DZHAY-kuhb |
| Judah | DZHOO-duh |
| Perez | PEE-rehz |
| Zerah | ZEE-ruh |
| Tamar | TAY-mer |

| | |
|---|---|
| Hezron | HEHZ-ruhn |
| Ram | RAM |
| Amminadab | ah-MIHN-uh-dab |
| Nahshon | NAH-shuhn |
| Salmon | SAL-muhn |
| Boaz | BO-az |
| Rahab | RAY-hab |
| Obed | O-behd |
| Jesse | DZHEH-see |
| Solomon | SAH-luh-muhn |
| Uriah | yoo-RAI-uh |
| Rehoboam | ree-ho-BO-am |
| Abijah | uh-BAI-dzhuh |
| Asaph | AY-saf |
| Jehoshaphat | dzhee-HAHSH-uh-fat |
| Joram | DZHO-ram |
| Uzziah | yoo-ZAI-uh |
| Jotham | DZHO-thuhm |
| Ahaz | AY-haz |
| Hezekiah | heh-zeh-KAI-uh |
| Manasseh | man-AS-eh |
| Amos | AY-muhs |
| Josiah | dzho-SAI-uh |
| Jechoniah | dzhehk-o-NAI-uh |
| Babylonian | bab-ih-LO-nih-uhn |
| Shealtiel | shee-AL-tih-ehl |
| Zerubbabel | zeh-RUH-buh-behl |
| Abiud | uh-BAI-uhd |

| | |
|---|---|
| Eliakim | ee-LAI-uh-kihm |
| Azor | AY-zawr |
| Zadok | ZAY-dahk |
| Achim | AY-kihm |
| Eliud | ee-LAI-uhd |
| Eleazar | ehl-ee-AY-zer |
| Matthan | MAT-than |
| Emmanuel | eh-MAN-yoo-ehl |

## CHRISTMAS — MIDNIGHT MASS

*First Reading*

| | |
|---|---|
| Midian | MIH-dih-uhn |

*Gospel*

| | |
|---|---|
| Caesar Augustus | SEE-zer uh-GUHS-tuhs |
| Quirinius | kwai-RIHN-ih-uhs |
| Syria | SIHR-ee-uh |
| Galilee | GAL-ih-lee |
| Nazareth | NAZ-uh-rehth |
| Judea | dzhoo-DEE-uh |
| Bethlehem | BEHTH-leh-hehm |
| Betrothed | bee-TRO*TH*D |
| Swaddling | SWAHD-lihng |

## CHRISTMAS — MASS AT DAWN

*First Reading*

| | |
|---|---|
| Zion | ZAI-uhn |

*Gospel*

| | |
|---|---|
| Bethlehem | BEHTH-leh-hehm |

## CHRISTMAS — MASS DURING THE DAY
*First Reading*

| | |
|---|---|
| Zion | ZAI-uhn |
| Jerusalem | dzheh-ROO-suh-lehm |

*Second Reading*

| | |
|---|---|
| Refulgence | ree-FOOL-dzhents |
| Purification | pyoor-ih-fih-KAY-shuhn |

## HOLY FAMILY
*Second Reading*

| | |
|---|---|
| Admonish | ad-MAH-nihsh |
| Psalms | SAHMZ |
| Hymns | HIHMZ |

*Gospel*

| | |
|---|---|
| Magi | MAY-dzhai |
| Herod | HEHR-uhd |
| Israel | IHZ-ray-ehl |
| Archelaus | ahr-kee-LAY-uhs |
| Judea | dzhoo-DEE-uh |
| Galilee | GAL-ih-lee |
| Nazareth | NAZ-uh-rehth |
| Nazorean | naz-aw-REE-uhn |

## JANUARY 1 — SOLEMNITY OF THE BLESSED VIRGIN MARY, THE MOTHER OF GOD
*First Reading*

| | |
|---|---|
| Aaron | EHR-uhn |
| Israelites | IHZ-rih-ehl-aits |

*Second Reading*
    Abba ------------- AB-uh
*Gospel*
    Bethlehem -------- BEHTH-leh-hehm
    Circumcision ----- ser-kuhm-SIHZH-uhn

## SECOND SUNDAY AFTER CHRISTMAS
*First Reading*
    Sirach ------------ SAI-rak
    Zion ------------- ZAI-uhn
*Second Reading*
    Ephesians --------- eh-FEE-zhuhnz

## THE EPIPHANY OF THE LORD
*First Reading*
    Jerusalem ---------- dzheh-ROO-suh-lehm
    Dromedaries ------ DRAH-muh-dehr-eez
    Midian ----------- MIH-dih-uhn
    Ephah ------------ EE-fuh
    Sheba ------------ SHEE-buh
    Frankincense ----- FRANGK-ihn-sehns
*Second Reading*
    Stewardship ------- STOO-erd-shihp
    Revelation -------- reh-veh-LAY-shuhn
    Gentiles ---------- DZHEHN-tailz
    Coheirs ----------- ko-EHRZ
*Gospel*
    Bethlehem -------- BEHTH-leh-hehm
    Judea ------------- dzhoo-DEE-uh

| | |
|---|---|
| Herod ------------ | HEHR-uhd |
| Magi ------------- | MAY-dzhai |
| Jerusalem ---------- | dzheh-ROO-suh-lehm |
| Judah ------------- | DZHOO-duh |
| Israel ------------- | IHZ-ray-ehl |
| Ascertained ------- | as-er-TAYND |
| Frankincense ----- | FRANGK-ihn-sehns |
| Myrrh ------------ | MER |

## THE BAPTISM OF THE LORD
*Second Reading*

| | |
|---|---|
| Cornelius ---------- | kawr-NEE-lee-uhs |
| Judea ------------- | dzhoo-DEE-uh |
| Galilee ------------ | GAL-ih-lee |
| Nazareth ---------- | NAZ-uh-rehth |

*Gospel*

| | |
|---|---|
| Galilee ------------ | GAL-ih-lee |
| Righteousness ----- | RAI-tshuhs-nehs |

## YEAR A
### Season of Lent

## ASH WEDNESDAY
*First Reading*

| | |
|---|---|
| Zion ------------- | ZAI-uhn |

*Second Reading*

| | |
|---|---|
| Ambassadors ------ | am-BAS-uh-derz |

*Gospel*
    Synagogues -------- SIHN-uh-gahgz
    Hypocrites -------- HIHP-uh-krihts

## FIRST SUNDAY OF LENT
*First Reading*
    Loincloths --------- LOIN-klaw*thz*
*Second Reading*
    Transgression ----- trans-GREHSH-uhn
    Condemnation --- kahn-dehm-NAY-shuhn
    Acquittal --------- uh-KWIHT'l
    Righteous -------- RAI-tshuhs
*Gospel*
    Parapet ----------- PEHR-uh-peht
    Prostrate ---------- PRAHS-trayt

## SECOND SUNDAY OF LENT
*First Reading*
    Abram ------------- AY-br'm
*Gospel*
    Elijah ------------- ee-LAI-dzhuh
    Prostrate ---------- PRAHS-trayt

## THIRD SUNDAY OF LENT
*First Reading*
    Massah ------------ MAH-suh
    Meribah ---------- MEHR-ih-bah
    Israelites ---------- IHZ-rih-ehl-aits

*Gospel*

| | |
|---|---|
| Samaria ------------ | suh-MEHR-ih-uh |
| Sychar ------------- | SAI-ker |
| Samaritan ---------- | suh-MEHR-ih-tuhn |
| Jerusalem ---------- | dzheh-ROO-suh-lehm |
| Messiah ------------ | meh-SAI-uh |
| Rabbi ------------- | RAB-ai |

## FOURTH SUNDAY IN LENT

*First Reading*

| | |
|---|---|
| Samuel ------------ | SAM-yoo-uhl |
| Eliab ------------- | ee-LAI-ab |
| Jesse ------------- | DZHEH-see |

*Gospel*

| | |
|---|---|
| Rabbi ------------- | RAB-ai |
| Siloam ------------ | sih-LO-uhm |
| Pharisees ---------- | FEHR-ih-seez |
| Sabbath ------------ | SAB-uhth |
| Synagogue --------- | SIHN-uh-gahg |

## FIFTH SUNDAY OF LENT

*First Reading*

| | |
|---|---|
| Israel ------------- | IHZ-ray-ehl |

*Second Reading*

| | |
|---|---|
| Righteousness ----- | RAI-tshuhs-nehs |

*Gospel*

| | |
|---|---|
| Lazarus ------------ | LAZ-er-uhs |
| Judea ------------- | dzhoo-DEE-uh |
| Didymus --------- | DIHD-ih-moos |

Bethany ---------- BEHTH-uh-nee

## PALM SUNDAY OF THE LORD'S PASSION

*Gospel at the Procession with Palms*

Jerusalem ---------- dzheh-ROO-suh-lehm
Bethphage -------- BEHTH-fuh-dzhee
Zion ------------- ZAI-uhn
Hosanna ---------- ho-ZAH-nuh
Nazareth ---------- NAZ-uh-rehth
Galilee ------------ GAL-ih-lee

*Gospel (Passion)*

Judas Iscariot ----- DZHOO-duhs
                     ihs-KEHR-ee-uht
Passover ---------- PAS-o-ver
Rabbi ------------ RAB-ai
Gethsemane ------ gehth-SEHM-uh-nee
Zebedee ---------- ZEH-beh-dee
Caiaphas ---------- KAY-uh-fuhs
Sanhedrin -------- san-HEE-drihn
Blasphemed ------ blas-FEEMD
Prophesy ---------- PRAH-feh-sai
Galilean ---------- gal-ih-LEE-uhn
Nazarene ---------- naz-uh-REEN
Pilate ------------- PAI-luht
Jeremiah ---------- dzhehr-eh-MAI-uh
Israelites ---------- IHZ-rih-ehl-aits
Barabbas ---------- buh-RAB-uhs
Praetorium ------- pray-TAWR-ih-uhm

| | |
|---|---|
| Cyrenian | sai-REE-nih-uhn |
| Golgotha | GAHL-guh-thuh |
| Eli, Eli, lema | AY-lee, AY-lee, luh-MAH |
| sabachthani | sah-bahk-TAH-nee |
| Elijah | ee-LAI-dzhuh |
| Magdalene | MAG-duh-lehn |
| Pharisees | FEHR-ih-seez |

## YEAR A

### Easter Triduum and Season of Easter

#### HOLY THURSDAY
*First Reading*

| | |
|---|---|
| Aaron | EHR-uhn |
| Israel | IHZ-ray-ehl |
| Procuring | pro-KYOOR-ihng |
| Passover | PAS-o-ver |

*Gospel*

| | |
|---|---|
| Passover | PAS-o-ver |
| Judas | DZHOO-duhs |
| Iscariot | ihs-KEHR-ee-uht |

#### GOOD FRIDAY
*First Reading*

| | |
|---|---|
| Chastisement | tshas-TAIZ-mehnt |
| Smitten | SMIHT'n |

*Second Reading*

| | |
|---|---|
| Supplications | suhp-lih-KAY-shuhnz |

*Gospel (Passion)*

| | |
|---|---|
| Kidron | KIHD-ruhn |
| Judas | DZHOO-duhs |
| Pharisees | FEHR-ih-seez |
| Nazarene | naz-uh-REEN |
| Malchus | MAL-kuhs |
| Annas | AN-uhs |
| Caiaphas | KAY-uh-fuhs |
| Synagogue | SIHN-uh-gahg |
| Praetorium | pray-TAWR-ih-uhm |
| Passover | PAS-o-ver |
| Pilate | PAI-luht |
| Barabbas | buh-RAB-uhs |
| Caesar | SEE-zer |
| Gabbatha | GAB-uh-thuh |
| Golgotha | GAHL-guh-thuh |
| Clopas | KLO-pas |
| Magdala | MAG-duh-luh |
| Hyssop | HIH-suhp |
| Arimathea | ehr-uh-muh-THEE-uh |
| Nicodemus | nih-ko-DEE-muhs |
| Myrrh | MER |
| Aloes | AL-oz |

## EASTER VIGIL

*First Reading*

| | |
|---|---|
| Abyss | uh-BIHS |
| Luminaries | LOO-mihn-ehr-eez |

*Second Reading*

| | |
|---|---|
| Abraham | AY-bruh-ham |
| Isaac | AI-zuhk |
| Moriah | maw-RAI-uh |
| Holocaust | HAHL-o-kawst |
| Yahweh-Yireh | YAH-weh-yer-AY |

*Third Reading*

| | |
|---|---|
| Israelites | IHZ-rih-ehl-aits |
| Pharaoh | FEHR-o |
| Charioteers | tsher-ih-uh-TEERS |
| Israel | IHZ-ray-ehl |

*Fourth Reading*

| | |
|---|---|
| Israel | IHZ-ray-ehl |
| Noah | NO-uh |
| Carnelians | kahr-NEEL-yuhnz |
| Sapphires | SAF-fai-erz |
| Carbuncles | KAHR-buhng-k'lz |

*Fifth Reading*

| | |
|---|---|
| Israel | IHZ-ray-ehl |

*Sixth Reading*

| | |
|---|---|
| Israel | IHZ-ray-ehl |
| Jacob | DZHAY-kuhb |
| Netherworld | NEH**TH**-er-werld |

*Seventh Reading*

| | |
|---|---|
| Profaned | pro-FAYND |
| Israel | IHZ-ray-ehl |

*Gospel*

| | |
|---|---|
| Magdalene | MAG-duh-lehn |
| Galilee | GAL-ih-lee |

## EASTER SUNDAY
*First Reading*

| | |
|---|---|
| Judea | dzhoo-DEE-uh |
| Galilee | GAL-ih-lee |
| Nazareth | NAZ-uh-rehth |
| Jerusalem | dzheh-ROO-suh-lehm |

*Second Reading*

| | |
|---|---|
| Unleavened | uhn-LEHV-uhnd |

*Gospel*

| | |
|---|---|
| Magdala | MAG-duh-luh |

*Gospel (used at Masses later in the day)*

| | |
|---|---|
| Jerusalem | dzheh-ROO-suh-lehm |
| Emmaus | eh-MAY-uhs |
| Cleopas | KLEE-o-pas |
| Nazarene | naz-uh-REEN |
| Israel | IHZ-ray-ehl |

## SECOND SUNDAY OF EASTER
*Gospel*

| | |
|---|---|
| Didymus | DIHD-ih-m*oo*s |

## THIRD SUNDAY OF EASTER
*First Reading*

| | |
|---|---|
| Jerusalem | dzheh-ROO-suh-lehm |
| Israelites | IHZ-rih-ehl-aits |
| Nazarene | naz-uh-REEN |

| | |
|---|---|
| Netherworld | NEH***TH***-er-werld |

*Second Reading*

| | |
|---|---|
| Sojourning | SO-dzhern-ihng |

*Gospel*

| | |
|---|---|
| Emmaus | eh-MAY-uhs |
| Cleopas | KLEE-o-pas |
| Jerusalem | dzheh-ROO-suh-lehm |
| Nazarene | naz-uh-REEN |
| Israel | IHZ-ray-ehl |

## FOURTH SUNDAY OF EASTER

*First Reading*

| | |
|---|---|
| Israel | IHZ-ray-ehl |
| Exhorting | ehg-ZORT-ihng |

*Gospel*

| | |
|---|---|
| Pharisees | FEHR-ih-seez |

## FIFTH SUNDAY OF EASTER

*First Reading*

| | |
|---|---|
| Hellenists | HEHL-uhn-ihsts |
| Hebrews | HEE-brooz |
| Prochorus | PRAH-kaw-ruhs |
| Nicanor | nai-KAY-nawr |
| Timon | TAI-muhn |
| Parmenas | PAHR-mee-nas |
| Antioch | AN-tih-ahk |
| Jerusalem | dzheh-ROO-suh-lehm |

*Second Reading*

| | |
|---|---|
| Zion | ZAI-uhn |

## Sixth Sunday of Easter
*First Reading*

| | |
|---|---|
| Samaria | suh-MEHR-ih-uh |
| Jerusalem | dzheh-ROO-suh-lehm |

*Second Reading*

| | |
|---|---|
| Sanctify | SANG-tih-fai |

## Ascension of the Lord
*First Reading*

| | |
|---|---|
| Theophilus | thee-AH-fih-luhs |
| Jerusalem | dzheh-ROO-suh-lehm |
| Israel | IHZ-ray-ehl |
| Judea | dzhoo-DEE-uh |
| Samaria | suh-MEHR-ih-uh |
| Galilee | GAL-ih-lee |

*Second Reading*

| | |
|---|---|
| Principality | prihn-sih-PAL-uh-tee |

*Gospel*

| | |
|---|---|
| Galilee | GAL-ih-lee |

## Seventh Sunday of Easter
*First Reading*

| | |
|---|---|
| Jerusalem | dzheh-ROO-suh-lehm |
| Olivet | AH-lih-veht |
| Bartholomew | bar-THAHL-uh-myoo |
| Alphaeus | AL-fee-uhs |
| Zealot | ZEH-laht |

*Second Reading*

| | |
|---|---|
| Exultantly | ehg-ZUHL-tent-lee |

## PENTECOST VIGIL
### First Reading

| | |
|---|---|
| Shinar | SHAI-nahr |
| Babel | BAY-b'l |
| Israelites | IHZ-rih-ehl-aits |
| Sinai | SAI-nai |
| Ezekiel | eh-ZEE-kee-'l |
| Sinews | SIHN-yooz |
| Israel | IHZ-ray-ehl |
| Zion | ZAI-uhn |
| Jerusalem | dzheh-ROO-suh-lehm |

## PENTECOST
### First Reading

| | |
|---|---|
| Pentecost | PEHN-tee-kawst |
| Galileans | gal-ih-LEE-uhnz |
| Parthians | PAHR-thee-uhnz |
| Medes | MEEDZ |
| Elamites | EE-luh-maits |
| Mesopotamia | mehs-uh-po-TAY-mih-uh |
| Judea | dzhoo-DEE-uh |
| Cappadocia | kap-uh-DO-shee-uh |
| Pontus | PAHN-tuhs |
| Phrygia | FRIH-dzhih-uh |
| Pamphylia | pam-FIHL-ih-uh |
| Libya | LIH-bih-uh |
| Cyrene | sai-REE-nee |

Judaism ------------ DZHOO-duh-ihz'm
Cretans ------------ KREE-tihnz

## YEAR A

### Ordinary Time

#### SECOND SUNDAY IN ORDINARY TIME
*First Reading*
Israel ------------- IHZ-ray-ehl
*Second Reading*
Sosthenes ---------- SAHS-thee-neez
Corinth ----------- KAWR-ihnth
*Gospel*
Israel ------------- IHZ-ray-ehl

#### THIRD SUNDAY IN ORDINARY TIME
*First Reading*
Zebulun ----------- ZEH-byoo-luhn
Nephtali ----------- NEHF-tih-lee
Gentiles ----------- DZHEHN-tailz
Midian ------------ MIH-dih-uhn
*Second Reading*
Chloe ------------- KLO-ee
Apollos ----------- uh-PAH-luhs
Cephas ----------- SEE-fuhs
*Gospel*
Galilee ------------ GAL-ih-lee

| | |
|---|---|
| Nazareth | NAZ-uh-rehth |
| Capernaum | kuh-PER-nay-uhm |
| Zebulun | ZEH-byoo-luhn |
| Nephtali | NEHF-tih-lee |
| Isaiah | ai-ZAY-uh |
| Gentiles | DZHEHN-tailz |
| Zebedee | ZEH-beh-dee |

## FOURTH SUNDAY IN ORDINARY TIME
*First Reading*

| | |
|---|---|
| Israel | IHZ-ray-ehl |

*Second Reading*

| | |
|---|---|
| Righteousness | RAI-tshuhs-nehs |
| Sanctification | sang-tih-fih-KAY-shuhn |
| Redemption | ree-DEHM-shuhn |

*Gospel*

| | |
|---|---|
| Righteousness | RAI-tshuhs-nehs |

## FIFTH SUNDAY IN ORDINARY TIME
*Second Reading*

| | |
|---|---|
| Sublimity | suhb-LIHM-ih-tee |

## SIXTH SUNDAY IN ORDINARY TIME
*Second Reading*

| | |
|---|---|
| Predetermined | pree-dee-TER-mihnd |

*Gospel*

| | |
|---|---|
| Pharisees | FEHR-ih-seez |
| Raga | RAH-guh |
| Sanhedrin | san-HEE-drihn |

| Gehenna | --------- | geh-HEHN-uh |
| Jerusalem | --------- | dzheh-ROO-suh-lehm |

## SEVENTH SUNDAY IN ORDINARY TIME

*First Reading*

| Leviticus | --------- | leh-VIH-tih-koos |
| Israelite | ----------- | IHZ-rih-ehl-ait |

*Second Reading*

| Corinthians | ------- | kawr-IHN-thee-uhnz |
| Apollos | ----------- | uh-PAH-luhs |
| Cephas | ----------- | SEE-fuhs |

## EIGHTH SUNDAY IN ORDINARY TIME

*First Reading*

| Isaiah | ------------- | ai-ZAY-uh |
| Zion | ------------- | ZAI-uhn |

*Second Reading*

| Corinthians | ------- | kawr-IHN-thee-uhnz |

*Gospel*

| Mammon | --------- | MAM-uhn |
| Righteousness | ---- | RAI-tshuhs-nehs |

## NINTH SUNDAY IN ORDINARY TIME

*First Reading*

| Deuteronomy | ---- | dyoo-ter-AH-nuh-mee |

*Second Reading*

| Righteousness | ---- | RAI-tshuhs-nehs |
| Expiation | --------- | ehks-pee-AY-shuhn |

## Tenth Sunday in Ordinary Time
*First Reading*

| | |
|---|---|
| Hosea | ho-ZEE-uh |
| Ephraim | EE-fray-ihm |
| Judah | DZHOO-duh |
| Holocausts | HAHL-o-kawsts |

*Second Reading*

| | |
|---|---|
| Righteousness | RAI-tshuhs-nehs |
| Transgressions | trans-GREHSH-uhnzs |

## Eleventh Sunday in Ordinary Time
*First Reading*

| | |
|---|---|
| Israelites | IHZ-rih-ehl-aits |
| Sinai | SAI-nai |

*Second Reading*

| | |
|---|---|
| Reconciliation | reh-kuhn-sih-lee-AY-shuhn |

*Gospel*

| | |
|---|---|
| Zebedee | ZEH-beh-dee |
| Bartholomew | bar-THAHL-uh-myoo |
| Alphaeus | AL-fee-uhs |
| Thaddeus | THAD-dee-uhs |
| Judas Iscariot | DZHOO-duhs ihs-KEHR-ee-uht |
| Samaritan | suh-MEHR-ih-tuhn |

## Twelfth Sunday in Ordinary Time
*First Reading*

| | |
|---|---|
| Jeremiah | dzhehr-eh-MAI-uh |

*Second Reading*
   Transgression ----- trans-GREHSH-uhn
*Gospel*
   Gehenna --------- geh-HEHN-uh

## THIRTEENTH SUNDAY IN ORDINARY TIME
*First Reading*
   Elisha ------------- ee-LAI-shuh
   Shunem ---------- SHOO-nehm
   Gehazi ------------ gee-HAY-zai

## FOURTEENTH SUNDAY IN ORDINARY TIME
*First Reading*
   Zion ------------- ZAI-uhn
   Jerusalem --------- dzheh-ROO-suh-lehm
   Ephraim ---------- EE-fray-ihm

## FIFTEENTH SUNDAY IN ORDINARY TIME
*Gospel*
   Parables ----------- PEHR-uh-buhlz

## SIXTEENTH SUNDAY IN ORDINARY TIME
*First Reading*
   Clemency --------- KLEHM-uhn-see
*Gospel*
   Leavened --------- LEHV-uhnd
   Parables ----------- PEHR-uh-buhlz

## SEVENTEENTH SUNDAY IN ORDINARY TIME
*First Reading*

Solomon ---------- SAH-luh-muhn

## EIGHTEENTH SUNDAY IN ORDINARY TIME
*First Reading*

Heedfully ---------- HEED-fool-ee

*Second Reading*

Principalities ------ prihn-sih-PAL-uh-teez

## NINETEENTH SUNDAY IN ORDINARY TIME
*First Reading*

Horeb ------------- HAWR-ehb

Elijah ------------- ee-LAI-dzhuh

*Second Reading*

Israelites ---------- IHZ-rih-ehl-aits

Patriarchs --------- PAY-trih-ahrks

## TWENTIETH SUNDAY IN ORDINARY TIME
*Gospel*

Tyre --------------- TAI-er

Sidon ------------- SAI-duhn

Canaanite --------- KAY-nuh-nait

## TWENTY-FIRST SUNDAY IN ORDINARY TIME
*First Reading*

Shebna ----------- SHEHB-nuh

Eliakim ----------- ee-LAI-uh-kihm

| | |
|---|---|
| Hilkiah ------------ | hihl-KAI-uh |
| Jerusalem ---------- | dzheh-ROO-suh-lehm |
| Judah -------------- | DZHOO-duh |

*Gospel*

| | |
|---|---|
| Caesarea Philippi-- | sehz-er-EE-uh fih-LIH-pai |
| Elijah -------------- | ee-LAI-dzhuh |
| Jeremiah ----------- | dzhehr-eh-MAI-uh |
| Jonah -------------- | DZHO-nuh |
| Netherworld ------ | NEH*TH*-er-werld |

## TWENTY-SECOND SUNDAY IN ORDINARY TIME

*Gospel*

| | |
|---|---|
| Jerusalem ---------- | dzheh-ROO-suh-lehm |

## TWENTY-THIRD SUNDAY IN ORDINARY TIME

*Gospel*

| | |
|---|---|
| Gentile ------------ | DZHEHN-tail |

## TWENTY-FOURTH SUNDAY IN ORDINARY TIME

*First Reading*

| | |
|---|---|
| Enmity ------------ | EHN-mih-tee |

## TWENTY-FIFTH SUNDAY IN ORDINARY TIME

*Gospel*

| | |
|---|---|
| Parable ------------ | PEHR-uh-buhl |

## TWENTY-SIXTH SUNDAY IN ORDINARY TIME
*Second Reading*
Vainglory ---------- VAYN-glaw-ree

## TWENTY-SEVENTH SUNDAY IN ORDINARY TIME
*First Reading*
Jerusalem ---------- dzheh-ROO-suh-lehm
Judah ------------- DZHOO-duh
Israel ------------- IHZ-ray-ehl
*Gospel*
Parable ----------- PEHR-uh-buhl

## TWENTY-EIGHTH SUNDAY IN ORDINARY TIME
*First Reading*
Isaiah ------------- ai-ZAY-uh
*Gospel*
Parables ----------- PEHR-uh-buhlz

## TWENTY-NINTH SUNDAY IN ORDINARY TIME
*First Reading*
Cyrus ------------ SAI-ruhs
Israel ------------- IHZ-ray-ehl
*Second Reading*
Silvanus------------ sihl-VAY-nuhs
Thessalonians ----- theh-suh-LO-nih-uhnz

*Gospel*

| | |
|---|---|
| Pharisees --------- | FEHR-ih-seez |
| Herodians -------- | hehr-O-dee-uhnz |
| Caesar ------------ | SEE-zer |

## THIRTIETH SUNDAY IN ORDINARY TIME

*Second Reading*

| | |
|---|---|
| Macedonia ------- | mas-eh-DO-nih-uh |
| Achaia ------------ | uh-KAY-yuh |

*Gospel*

| | |
|---|---|
| Pharisees --------- | FEHR-ih-seez |
| Sadducees -------- | SAD-dzhoo-seez |

## THIRTY-FIRST SUNDAY IN ORDINARY TIME

*First Reading*

| | |
|---|---|
| Levi -------------- | LEE-vai |

*Gospel*

| | |
|---|---|
| Pharisees --------- | FEHR-ih-seez |
| Phylacteries ------- | fih-LAK-ter-eez |
| Synagogues ------- | SIHN-uh-gahgz |
| Rabbi ------------ | RAB-ai |

## THIRTY-SECOND SUNDAY IN ORDINARY TIME

*First Reading*

| | |
|---|---|
| Solicitude --------- | so-LIHS-ih-tyood |

*Second Reading*

| | |
|---|---|
| Archangel -------- | AHRK-ayn-dzhul |

**THIRTY-THIRD SUNDAY IN ORDINARY TIME**
*Gospel*
    Disciples ---------- dih-SAI-p'lz
    Parable ----------- PEHR-uh-buhl

**CHRIST THE KING**
*Second Reading*
    Sovereignty ------- SAH-vrehn-tee

## YEAR A

### Solemnities of the Lord During Ordinary Time

**THE SOLEMNITY OF THE MOST HOLY TRINITY**
*First Reading*
    Sinai--------------- SAI-nai

**THE SOLEMNITY OF THE MOST HOLY BODY AND BLOOD OF CHRIST**
*First Reading*
    Manna------------- MAN-uh

# YEAR A

## Other Solemnities

### DECEMBER 8 — THE IMMACULATE CONCEPTION OF THE BLESSED VIRGIN MARY

*First Reading*

| | |
|---|---|
| Enmity | EHN-mih-tee |

*Gospel*

| | |
|---|---|
| Gabriel | GAY-bree-'l |
| Galilee | GAL-ih-lee |
| Nazareth | NAZ-uh-rehth |
| Jacob | DZHAY-kuhb |

### AUGUST 15 — THE ASSUMPTION OF THE BLESSED VIRGIN MARY

## Assumption Vigil

*First Reading*

| | |
|---|---|
| Israel | IHZ-ray-ehl |
| Jerusalem | dzheh-ROO-suh-lehm |
| Aaron | EHR-uhn |
| Levites | LEE-vaits |
| Lyres | LAI-erz |
| Cymbals | SIHM-b'lz |

*Second Reading*
   Immortality ------- ih-mor-TAL-ih-tee

## Assumption
*First Reading*
   Diadem ----------- DAI-uh-dehm
*Second Reading*
   Sovereignty ------- SAH-vrehn-tee
*Gospel*
   Judah ------------- DZHOO-duh
   Zechariah -------- zeh-kuh-RAI-uh
   Israel ------------- IHZ-ray-ehl
   Abraham --------- AY-bruh-ham

## NOVEMBER 1 — ALL SAINTS
*First Reading*
   Israelites ---------- IHZ-rih-ehl-aits
   Prostrated--------- PRAHS-trayt-ehd
*Gospel*
   Righteousness ---- RAI-tshuhs-nehs

## YEAR B

### Season of Advent

**FIRST SUNDAY OF ADVENT**
*Second Reading*

Irreproachable ---- eer-ih-PROTSH-uh-b'l

**SECOND SUNDAY OF ADVENT**
*First Reading*

Jerusalem --------- dzheh-ROO-suh-lehm
Zion ------------- ZAI-uhn
Expiated ---------- EHKS-pee-ayt-ehd
Judah ------------- DZHOO-duh
Recompense ----- REH-kuhm-pehns

*Gospel*

Isaiah ------------- ai-ZAY-uh
Judean ------------ dzhoo-DEE-uhn
Jerusalem --------- dzheh-ROO-suh-lehm

**THIRD SUNDAY OF ADVENT**
*First Reading*

Diadem ----------- DAI-uh-dehm

*Gospel*

Jerusalem --------- dzheh-ROO-suh-lehm
Elijah ------------- ee-LAI-dzhuh

| Isaiah | ai-ZAY-uh |
|--------|-----------|
| Pharisees | FEHR-ih-seez |
| Bethany | BEHTH-uh-nee |

## FOURTH SUNDAY OF ADVENT
*First Reading*

| Israel | IHZ-ray-ehl |
|--------|-------------|

*Gospel*

| Gabriel | GAY-bree-'l |
|---------|-------------|
| Galilee | GAL-ih-lee |
| Nazareth | NAZ-uh-rehth |
| Jacob | DZHAY-kuhb |

---

## YEAR B
### Season of Christmas

## CHRISTMAS — VIGIL MASS
*First Reading*

| Zion | ZAI-uhn |
|------|---------|
| Jerusalem | dzheh-ROO-suh-lehm |
| Vindication | vihn-dih-KAY-shuhn |
| Diadem | DAI-uh-dehm |
| Espoused | eh-SPAUZD |

*Second Reading*

| Antioch | AN-tih-ahk |
|---------|-----------|
| Pisidia | pih-SIH-dih-uh |
| Synagogue | SIHN-uh-gahg |
| Israelites | IHZ-rih-ehl-aits |

Israel ------------- IHZ-ray-ehl
Sojourn ---------- SO-dzhern
Jesse ------------- DZHEH-see

*Gospel*

Genealogy -------- dzhee-nee-AH-lo-dzhee
Abraham --------- AY-bruh-ham
Isaac ------------- AI-zuhk
Jacob ------------- DZHAY-kuhb
Judah ------------- DZHOO-duh
Perez ------------- PEE-rehz
Zerah ------------- ZEE-ruh
Tamar ------------- TAY-mer
Hezron ----------- HEHZ-ruhn
Ram ------------- RAM
Amminadab ------ ah-MIHN-uh-dab
Nahshon ---------- NAH-shuhn
Salmon ----------- SAL-muhn
Boaz ------------- BO-az
Rahab ------------ RAY-hab
Obed ------------- O-behd
Jesse ------------- DZHEH-see
Solomon ---------- SAH-luh-muhn
Uriah ------------- y**oo**-RAI-uh
Rehoboam ------- ree-ho-BO-am
Abijah ------------ uh-BAI-dzhuh
Asaph ------------ AY-saf
Jehoshaphat ------- dzhee-HAHSH-uh-fat
Joram ------------- DZHO-ram

| | |
|---|---|
| Uzziah | yoo-ZAI-uh |
| Jotham | DZHO-thuhm |
| Ahaz | AY-haz |
| Hezekiah | heh-zeh-KAI-uh |
| Manasseh | man-AS-eh |
| Amos | AY-muhs |
| Josiah | dzho-SAI-uh |
| Jechoniah | dzhehk-o-NAI-uh |
| Babylonian | bab-ih-LO-nih-uhn |
| Shealtiel | shee-AL-tih-ehl |
| Zerubbabel | zeh-RUH-buh-behl |
| Abiud | uh-BAI-uhd |
| Eliakim | ee-LAI-uh-kihm |
| Azor | AY-zawr |
| Zadok | ZAY-dahk |
| Achim | AY-kihm |
| Eliud | ee-LAI-uhd |
| Eleazar | ehl-ee-AY-zer |
| Matthan | MAT-than |
| Emmanuel | eh-MAN-yoo-ehl |

## CHRISTMAS — MIDNIGHT MASS
*First Reading*

| | |
|---|---|
| Midian | MIH-dih-uhn |

*Gospel*

| | |
|---|---|
| Caesar Augustus | SEE-zer uh-GUHS-tuhs |
| Quirinius | kwai-RIHN-ih-uhs |

| | |
|---|---|
| Syria | SIHR-ee-uh |
| Galilee | GAL-ih-lee |
| Nazareth | NAZ-uh-rehth |
| Judea | dzhoo-DEE-uh |
| Bethlehem | BEHTH-leh-hehm |
| Betrothed | bee-TRO*TH*D |
| Swaddling | SWAHD-lihng |

## CHRISTMAS — MASS AT DAWN
*First Reading*

| | |
|---|---|
| Zion | ZAI-uhn |

*Gospel*

| | |
|---|---|
| Bethlehem | BEHTH-leh-hehm |

## CHRISTMAS — MASS DURING THE DAY
*First Reading*

| | |
|---|---|
| Zion | ZAI-uhn |
| Jerusalem | dzheh-ROO-suh-lehm |

*Second Reading*

| | |
|---|---|
| Refulgence | ree-FOOL-dzhents |
| Purification | pyoor-ih-fih-KAY-shuhn |

## HOLY FAMILY
*First Reading*

| | |
|---|---|
| Abram | AY-br'm |
| Righteousness | RAI-tshuhs-nehs |
| Abraham | AY-bruh-ham |
| Isaac | AI-zuhk |

*Second Reading*

| | |
|---|---|
| Abraham | AY-bruh-ham |
| Isaac | AI-zuhk |

*Gospel*

| | |
|---|---|
| Jerusalem | dzheh-ROO-suh-lehm |
| Purification | pyoor-ih-fih-KAY-shuhn |
| Simeon | SIHM-ee-uhn |
| Israel | IHZ-ray-ehl |
| Gentiles | DZHEHN-tailz |
| Phanuel | FAN-yoo-ehl |
| Asher | ASH-er |
| Galilee | GAL-ih-lee |
| Nazareth | NAZ-uh-rehth |

## SOLEMNITY OF THE BLESSED VIRGIN MARY, THE MOTHER OF GOD

*First Reading*

| | |
|---|---|
| Aaron | EHR-uhn |
| Israelites | IHZ-rih-ehl-aits |

*Second Reading*

| | |
|---|---|
| Abba | AB-uh |

*Gospel*

| | |
|---|---|
| Bethlehem | BEHTH-leh-hehm |
| Circumcision | ser-kuhm-SIHZH-uhn |

## SECOND SUNDAY AFTER CHRISTMAS
*First Reading*

| | |
|---|---|
| Sirach | SAI-rak |
| Zion | ZAI-uhn |

*Second Reading*

| | |
|---|---|
| Ephesians | eh-FEE-zhuhnz |

## THE EPIPHANY OF THE LORD
*First Reading*

| | |
|---|---|
| Jerusalem | dzheh-ROO-suh-lehm |
| Dromedaries | DRAH-muh-dehr-eez |
| Midian | MIH-dih-uhn |
| Ephah | EE-fuh |
| Sheba | SHEE-buh |
| Frankincense | FRANGK-ihn-sehns |

*Second Reading*

| | |
|---|---|
| Stewardship | STOO-erd-shihp |
| Revelation | reh-veh-LAY-shuhn |
| Gentiles | DZHEHN-tailz |
| Coheirs | ko-EHRZ |

*Gospel*

| | |
|---|---|
| Bethlehem | BEHTH-leh-hehm |
| Judea | dzhoo-DEE-uh |
| Herod | HEHR-uhd |
| Magi | MAY-dzhai |

| Jerusalem | dzheh-ROO-suh-lehm |
|-----------|--------------------|
| Judah | DZHOO-duh |
| Israel | IHZ-ray-ehl |
| Ascertained | as-er-TAYND |
| Frankincense | FRANGK-ihn-sehns |
| Myrrh | MER |

## THE BAPTISM OF THE LORD
*Second Reading*

| Cornelius | kawr-NEE-lee-uhs |
|-----------|------------------|
| Judea | dzhoo-DEE-uh |
| Galilee | GAL-ih-lee |
| Nazareth | NAZ-uh-rehth |

*Gospel*

| Nazareth | NAZ-uh-rehth |
|----------|--------------|
| Galilee | GAL-ih-lee |

## YEAR B

### Season of Lent

## ASH WEDNESDAY
*First Reading*

| Zion | ZAI-uhn |
|------|---------|

*Second Reading*

| Ambassadors | am-BAS-uh-derz |
|-------------|----------------|

*Gospel*
   Synagogues -------- SIHN-uh-gahgz
   Hypocrites -------- HIHP-uh-krihts

## First Sunday of Lent
*First Reading*
   Noah ------------- NO-uh
*Second Reading*
   Noah ------------- NO-uh
*Gospel*
   Galilee ------------ GAL-ih-lee

## Second Sunday of Lent
*First Reading*
   Abraham --------- AY-bruh-ham
   Isaac -------------- AI-zuhk
   Moriah ----------- maw-RAI-uh
*Gospel*
   Elijah ------------- ee-LAI-dzhuh
   Rabbi ------------- RAB-ai

## Third Sunday of Lent
*Second Reading*
   Gentiles ---------- DZHEHN-tailz
*Gospel*
   Passover ---------- PAS-o-ver
   Jerusalem --------- dzheh-ROO-suh-lehm

## FOURTH SUNDAY OF LENT
*First Reading*

| | |
|---|---|
| Judah | DZHOO-duh |
| Jerusalem | dzheh-ROO-suh-lehm |
| Babylon | BAB-ih-luhn |
| Chaldeans | kal-DEE-uhnz |
| Persians | PER-zhuhnz |
| Jeremiah | dzhehr-eh-MAI-uh |
| Cyrus | SAI-ruhs |

*Gospel*

| | |
|---|---|
| Nicodemus | nih-ko-DEE-muhs |

## FIFTH SUNDAY OF LENT
*First Reading*

| | |
|---|---|
| Israel | IHZ-ray-ehl |
| Judah | DZHOO-duh |

*Gospel*

| | |
|---|---|
| Passover | PAS-o-ver |
| Bethsaida | behth-SAY-ih-duh |
| Galilee | GAL-ih-lee |

## PALM SUNDAY OF THE LORD'S PASSION
*Gospel at the Procession with Palms*

| | |
|---|---|
| Jerusalem | dzheh-ROO-suh-lehm |
| Bethphage | BEHTH-fuh-dzhee |
| Bethany | BEHTH-uh-nee |

| | |
|---|---|
| Hosanna ---------- | ho-ZAH-nuh |
| Zion ------------- | ZAI-uhn |

*Gospel (Passion)*

| | |
|---|---|
| Passover ---------- | PAS-o-ver |
| Bethany ---------- | BEHTH-uh-nee |
| Simon ------------ | SAI-muhn |
| Alabaster --------- | al-uh-BAS-ter |
| Spikenard --------- | SPAIK-nahrd |
| Judas Iscariot ----- | DZHOO-duhs |
| | ihs-KEHR-ee-uht |
| Galilee ------------ | GAL-ih-lee |
| Gethsemane ------- | gehth-SEHM-uh-nee |
| Abba ------------- | AB-uh |
| Rabbi ------------ | RAB-ai |
| Sanhedrin --------- | san-HEE-drihn |
| Blasphemy -------- | BLAS-fuh-mee |
| Nazarene --------- | naz-uh-REEN |
| Galilean ---------- | gal-ih-LEE-uhn |
| Pilate ------------ | PAI-luht |
| Barabbas ---------- | buh-RAB-uhs |
| Cyrenian --------- | sai-REE-nih-uhn |
| Rufus ------------ | ROO-fuhs |
| Golgotha --------- | GAHL-guh-thuh |
| Eloi, Eloi, --------- | AY-lo-ee, AY-lo-ee, |
| lema ----------- | luh-MAH |
| sabachthani ---- | sah-bahk-TAH-nee |

| | |
|---|---|
| Elijah | ee-LAI-dzhuh |
| Magdalene | MAG-duh-lehn |
| Joses | DZHO-seez |
| Salome | suh-LO-mee |
| Arimathea | ehr-uh-muh-THEE-uh |
| Centurion | sehn-TSHOOR-ee-uhn |

# YEAR B

## Easter Triduum and Season of Easter

### HOLY THURSDAY
*First Reading*

| | |
|---|---|
| Aaron | EHR-uhn |
| Israel | IHZ-ray-ehl |
| Procuring | pro-KYOOR-ihng |
| Passover | PAS-o-ver |

*Gospel*

| | |
|---|---|
| Passover | PAS-o-ver |
| Judas | DZHOO-duhs |
| Iscariot | ihs-KEHR-ee-uht |

### GOOD FRIDAY
*First Reading*

| | |
|---|---|
| Chastisement | tshas-TAIZ-mehnt |
| Smitten | SMIHT'n |

*Second Reading*
   Supplications ----- suhp-lih-KAY-shuhnz
*Gospel (Passion)*
   Kidron ------------ KIHD-ruhn
   Judas -------------- DZHOO-duhs
   Pharisees --------- FEHR-ih-seez
   Nazarene --------- naz-uh-REEN
   Malchus ----------- MAL-kuhs
   Annas ------------- AN-uhs
   Caiaphas ----------- KAY-uh-fuhs
   Synagogue --------- SIHN-uh-gahg
   Praetorium ------- pray-TAWR-ih-uhm
   Passover ----------- PAS-o-ver
   Pilate -------------- PAI-luht
   Barabbas ----------- buh-RAB-uhs
   Caesar ------------- SEE-zer
   Gabbatha --------- GAB-uh-thuh
   Golgotha --------- GAHL-guh-thuh
   Clopas ------------- KLO-pas
   Magdala ----------- MAG-duh-luh
   Hyssop ------------ HIH-suhp
   Arimathea -------- ehr-uh-muh-THEE-uh
   Nicodemus ------- nih-ko-DEE-muhs
   Myrrh ------------- MER
   Aloes -------------- AL-oz

## EASTER VIGIL
### First Reading
| | |
|---|---|
| Abyss | uh-BIHS |
| Luminaries | LOO-mihn-ehr-eez |

### Second Reading
| | |
|---|---|
| Abraham | AY-bruh-ham |
| Isaac | AI-zuhk |
| Moriah | maw-RAI-uh |
| Holocaust | HAHL-o-kawst |
| Yahweh-Yireh | YAH-weh-yer-AY |

### Third Reading
| | |
|---|---|
| Israelites | IHZ-rih-ehl-aits |
| Pharaoh | FEHR-o |
| Charioteers | tsher-ih-uh-TEERS |
| Israel | IHZ-ray-ehl |

### Fourth Reading
| | |
|---|---|
| Israel | IHZ-ray-ehl |
| Noah | NO-uh |
| Carnelians | kahr-NEEL-yuhnz |
| Sapphires | SAF-fai-erz |
| Carbuncles | KAHR-buhng-k'lz |

### Fifth Reading
| | |
|---|---|
| Israel | IHZ-ray-ehl |

### Sixth Reading
| | |
|---|---|
| Israel | IHZ-ray-ehl |
| Jacob | DZHAY-kuhb |
| Netherworld | NEH**TH**-er-werld |

*Seventh Reading*

| | |
|---|---|
| Profaned | pro-FAYND |
| Israel | IHZ-ray-ehl |

*Gospel*

| | |
|---|---|
| Magdalene | MAG-duh-lehn |
| Salome | suh-LO-mee |
| Nazareth | NAZ-uh-rehth |
| Galilee | GAL-ih-lee |

## EASTER SUNDAY

*First Reading*

| | |
|---|---|
| Judea | dzhoo-DEE-uh |
| Galilee | GAL-ih-lee |
| Nazareth | NAZ-uh-rehth |
| Jerusalem | dzheh-ROO-suh-lehm |

*Second Reading*

| | |
|---|---|
| Paschal | PAS-k'l |

*Gospel*

| | |
|---|---|
| Magdala | MAG-duh-luh |

*Gospel (used at Masses later in the day)*

| | |
|---|---|
| Jerusalem | dzheh-ROO-suh-lehm |
| Emmaus | eh-MAY-uhs |
| Cleopas | KLEE-o-pas |
| Nazarene | naz-uh-REEN |
| Israel | IHZ-ray-ehl |

## SECOND SUNDAY OF EASTER

*Gospel*

| | |
|---|---|
| Didymus | DIHD-ih-moos |

## THIRD SUNDAY OF EASTER
*First Reading*

| | |
|---|---|
| Isaac | AI-zuhk |

*Gospel*

| | |
|---|---|
| Jerusalem | dzheh-ROO-suh-lehm |

## FOURTH SUNDAY OF EASTER
*First Reading*

| | |
|---|---|
| Israel | IHZ-ray-ehl |
| Nazarene | naz-uh-REEN |

## FIFTH SUNDAY OF EASTER
*First Reading*

| | |
|---|---|
| Jerusalem | dzheh-ROO-suh-lehm |
| Barnabas | BAHR-nuh-buhs |
| Damascus | duh-MAS-kuhs |
| Hellenists | HEHL-uhn-ihsts |
| Caesarea | sehz-er-EE-uh |
| Tarsus | TAHR-suhs |
| Judea | dzhoo-DEE-uh |
| Galilee | GAL-ih-lee |
| Samaria | suh-MEHR-ih-uh |

## SIXTH SUNDAY OF EASTER
*First Reading*

| | |
|---|---|
| Cornelius | kawr-NEE-lee-uhs |
| Circumcised | ser-kuhm-SAIZD |
| Gentiles | DZHEHN-tailz |

*Second Reading*
  Expiation ---------- ehks-pee-AY-shuhn

## THE ASCENSION OF THE LORD
*First Reading*
  Theophilus ------- thee-AH-fih-luhs
  Jerusalem ---------- dzheh-ROO-suh-lehm
  Judea -------------- dzhoo-DEE-uh
  Samaria ----------- suh-MEHR-ih-uh
  Galilee ------------ GAL-ih-lee

## SEVENTH SUNDAY OF EASTER
*First Reading*
  Judas -------------- DZHOO-duhs
  Psalms ------------ SAHMZ
  Barsabbas --------- BAHR-suh-buhs
  Justus ------------- DZHUHS-tuhs
  Matthias ---------- muh-THAI-uhs

## PENTECOST — VIGIL
*First Reading*
  Shinar ------------ SHAI-nahr
  Bitumen ---------- bih-TYOO-m'n
  Babel ------------- BAY-b'l
  Jacob -------------- DZHAY-kuhb
  Israelites ---------- IHZ-rih-ehl-aits
  Egyptians --------- ee-DZHIHP-shuhnz
  Sinai -------------- SAI-nai

| Israel | IHZ-ray-ehl |
| Prophesy | PRAH-feh-sai |
| Zion | ZAI-uhn |
| Jerusalem | dzheh-ROO-suh-lehm |

## PENTECOST
### First Reading

| Galileans | gal-ih-LEE-uhnz |
| Parthians | PAHR-thee-uhnz |
| Medes | MEEDZ |
| Elamites | EE-luh-maits |
| Mesopotamia | mehs-uh-po-TAY-mih-uh |
| Judea | dzhoo-DEE-uh |
| Cappadocia | kap-uh-DO-shee-uh |
| Pontus | PAHN-tuhs |
| Phrygia | FRIH-dzhih-uh |
| Pamphylia | pam-FIHL-ih-uh |
| Libya | LIH-bih-uh |
| Cyrene | sai-REE-nee |
| Judaism | DZHOO-duh-ihz'm |
| Cretans | KREE-tihnz |

# YEAR B
## Ordinary Time

### SECOND SUNDAY IN ORDINARY TIME
*First Reading*

| | |
|---|---|
| Samuel | SAM-yoo-uhl |
| Eli | EE-lai |

*Gospel*

| | |
|---|---|
| Rabbi | RAB-ai |
| Simon | SAI-muhn |
| Messiah | meh-SAI-uh |
| Cephas | SEE-fuhs |

### THIRD SUNDAY IN ORDINARY TIME
*First Reading*

| | |
|---|---|
| Jonah | DZHO-nuh |
| Nineveh | NIHN-eh-veh |

*Gospel*

| | |
|---|---|
| Galilee | GAL-ih-lee |
| Zebedee | ZEH-beh-dee |

### FOURTH SUNDAY IN ORDINARY TIME
*Gospel*

| | |
|---|---|
| Capernaum | kuh-PER-nay-uhm |
| Synagogue | SIHN-uh-gahg |
| Nazareth | NAZ-uh-rehth |
| Galilee | GAL-ih-lee |

## FIFTH SUNDAY IN ORDINARY TIME
*Gospel*

Synagogue --------- SIHN-uh-gahg

## SIXTH SUNDAY IN ORDINARY TIME
*First Reading*

Aaron ------------ EHR-uhn
Leprous ----------- LEHP-ruhs
Leprosy ----------- LEHP-ruh-see

*Gospel*

Leprosy ----------- LEHP-ruh-see

## SEVENTH SUNDAY IN ORDINARY TIME
*First Reading*

Jacob ------------- DZHAY-kuhb
Israel ------------- IHZ-ray-ehl

*Second Reading*

Silvanus ----------- sihl-VAY-nuhs

*Gospel*

Capernaum ------- kuh-PER-nay-uhm

## EIGHTH SUNDAY IN ORDINARY TIME
*Gospel*

Pharisees --------- FEHR-ih-seez

## NINTH SUNDAY IN ORDINARY TIME
*Gospel*

Pharisees --------- FEHR-ih-seez

Abiathar ----------- uh-BAI-uh-ther
Herodians -------- hehr-O-dee-uhnz

## TENTH SUNDAY IN ORDINARY TIME
*First Reading*
Enmity ----------- EHN-mih-tee
*Gospel*
Beelzebul --------- bee-EHL-zee-buhl

## ELEVENTH SUNDAY IN ORDINARY TIME
*First Reading*
Ezekiel ----------- eh-ZEE-kee-'l
Israel ------------- IHZ-ray-ehl

## TWELFTH SUNDAY IN ORDINARY TIME
*First Reading*
Job --------------- DZHOB

## THIRTEENTH SUNDAY IN ORDINARY TIME
*Gospel*
Synagogue --------- SIHN-uh-gahg
Jairus ------------- DZHAI-*roo*s
Hemorrhages ----- HEHM-uh-rihdzh'z
Talitha Koum ----- TAL-ih-thuh KOOM

## FOURTEENTH SUNDAY IN ORDINARY TIME
*First Reading*
Israelites ---------- IHZ-rih-ehl-aits

*Gospel*
| | |
|---|---|
| Synagogue | SIHN-uh-gahg |
| Joses | DZHO-seez |
| Judas | DZHOO-duhs |

## FIFTEENTH SUNDAY IN ORDINARY TIME
*First Reading*
| | |
|---|---|
| Amaziah | am-uh-ZAI-uh |
| Bethel | BETH'l |
| Prophesy | PRAH-feh-sai |

## SIXTEENTH SUNDAY IN ORDINARY TIME
*First Reading*
| | |
|---|---|
| Israel | IHZ-ray-ehl |
| Judah | DZHOO-duh |

*Second Reading*
| | |
|---|---|
| Enmity | EHN-mih-tee |

## SEVENTEENTH SUNDAY IN ORDINARY TIME
*First Reading*
| | |
|---|---|
| Baal-Shalishah | BAY-uhl-shuh-LAI-shuh |
| Elisha | ee-LAI-shuh |

*Gospel*
| | |
|---|---|
| Galilee | GAL-ih-lee |
| Passover | PAS-o-ver |

## EIGHTEENTH SUNDAY IN ORDINARY TIME
*First Reading*
| | |
|---|---|
| Israelites | IHZ-rih-ehl-aits |

*Gospel*

| | |
|---|---|
| Capernaum | kuh-PER-nay-uhm |

## NINETEENTH SUNDAY IN ORDINARY TIME
*First Reading*

| | |
|---|---|
| Elijah | ee-LAI-dzhuh |
| Horeb | HAWR-ehb |

## TWENTIETH SUNDAY IN ORDINARY TIME
*Second Reading*

| | |
|---|---|
| Ephesians | eh-FEE-zhuhnz |

## TWENTY-FIRST SUNDAY IN ORDINARY TIME
*First Reading*

| | |
|---|---|
| Joshua | DZHAH-shoo-uh |
| Israel | IHZ-ray-ehl |
| Shechem | SHEE-kehm |
| Amorites | AM-uh-raits |
| Egypt | EE-dzhihpt |

## TWENTY-SECOND SUNDAY IN ORDINARY TIME
*First Reading*

| | |
|---|---|
| Israel | IHZ-ray-ehl |

*Gospel*

| | |
|---|---|
| Pharisees | FEHR-ih-seez |
| Jerusalem | dzheh-ROO-suh-lehm |
| Isaiah | ai-ZAY-uh |
| Prophesy | PRAH-feh-sai |
| Hypocrites | HIHP-uh-krihts |

Licentiousness ---- lai-SEHN-shuhs-nihs
Blasphemy -------- BLAS-fuh-mee

## TWENTY-THIRD SUNDAY IN ORDINARY TIME
*Gospel*

Tyre -------------- TAI-er
Sidon ------------- SAI-duhn
Galilee ------------ GAL-ih-lee
Decapolis --------- dee-KAP-o-lihs
Ephphatha -------- EHF-uh-thuh

## TWENTY-FOURTH SUNDAY IN ORDINARY TIME
*Gospel*

Caesarea Philippi-- sehz-er-EE-uh
fih-LIH-pai
Elijah ------------- ee-LAI-dzhuh

## TWENTY-FIFTH SUNDAY IN ORDINARY TIME
*Second Reading*

Righteousness ---- RAI-tshuhs-nehs
*Gospel*

Galilee ------------ GAL-ih-lee
Disciples ---------- dih-SAI-p'lz
Capernaum ------- kuh-PER-nay-uhm

## TWENTY-SIXTH SUNDAY IN ORDINARY TIME
*First Reading*

Prophesied-------- PRAH-feh-said
Eldad ------------- EHL-dad

| | |
|---|---|
| Medad | MEE-dad |
| Joshua | DZHAH-shoo-uh |
| Nun | NUHN |

*Gospel*

| | |
|---|---|
| Gehenna | geh-HEHN-uh |

## TWENTY-SEVENTH SUNDAY IN ORDINARY TIME

*Second Reading*

| | |
|---|---|
| Consecrated | KAHN-seh-kray-tehd |

*Gospel*

| | |
|---|---|
| Pharisees | FEHR-ih-seez |

## TWENTY-EIGHTH SUNDAY IN ORDINARY TIME

*First Reading*

| | |
|---|---|
| Scepter | SEHP-ter |
| Mire | MAI-er |

*Second Reading*

| | |
|---|---|
| Marrow | MEHR-o |

## TWENTY-NINTH SUNDAY IN ORDINARY TIME

*Gospel*

| | |
|---|---|
| Zebedee | ZEH-beh-dee |
| Gentiles | DZHEHN-tailz |

## THIRTIETH SUNDAY IN ORDINARY TIME

*First Reading*

| | |
|---|---|
| Israel | IHZ-ray-ehl |
| Ephraim | EE-fray-ihm |

*Second Reading*
    Aaron ------------- EHR-uhn
    Melchizedek ------ mehl-KIHZ-eh-dehk
*Gospel*
    Jericho ------------ DZHEHR-ih-ko
    Bartimaeus ------- bar-tih-MEE-uhs
    Timaeus ----------- tai-MEE-uhs
    Nazareth --------- NAZ-uh-rehth

## THIRTY-FIRST SUNDAY IN ORDINARY TIME
*First Reading*
    Israel -------------- IHZ-ray-ehl
*Second Reading*
    Levitical ---------- leh-VIH-tih-k'l

## THIRTY-SECOND SUNDAY IN ORDINARY TIME
*First Reading*
    Elijah -------------- ee-LAI-dzhuh
    Zarephath --------- ZEHR-ee-fath
    Israel -------------- IHZ-ray-ehl
*Second Reading*
    Sanctuary ---------- SANG-tshoo-ehr-ee
*Gospel*
    Synagogues ------- SIHN-uh-gahgz

## THIRTY-THIRD SUNDAY IN ORDINARY TIME
*Gospel*
    Tribulation ------- trihb-yoo-LAY-shuhn

## CHRIST THE KING
*Second Reading*
    Alpha ------------- AHL-fuh
    Omega ------------ o-MAY-guh
*Gospel*
    Pilate ------------- PAI-luht

---
## YEAR B
### Solemnities of the Lord During Ordinary Time

## THE SOLEMNITY OF THE MOST HOLY TRINITY
*Second Reading*
    Abba ------------- AB-uh
*Gospel*
    Galilee ------------ GAL-ih-lee

## THE SOLEMNITY OF THE MOST HOLY BODY AND BLOOD OF CHRIST
*First Reading*
    Israel ------------- IHZ-ray-ehl

| | |
|---|---|
| Israelites | IHZ-rih-ehl-aits |
| Holocausts | HAHL-o-kawsts |

*Second Reading*

| | |
|---|---|
| Heifer | HEH-fer |

*Gospel*

| | |
|---|---|
| Passover | PAS-o-ver |

## YEAR B

### Other Solemnities

## DECEMBER 8 — THE IMMACULATE CONCEPTION OF THE BLESSED VIRGIN MARY

*First Reading*

| | |
|---|---|
| Enmity | EHN-mih-tee |

*Gospel*

| | |
|---|---|
| Gabriel | GAY-bree-'l |
| Galilee | GAL-ih-lee |
| Nazareth | NAZ-uh-rehth |
| Jacob | DZHAY-kuhb |

## AUGUST 15 — THE ASSUMPTION OF THE BLESSED VIRGIN MARY

## Assumption Vigil

*First Reading*

| | |
|---|---|
| Israel | IHZ-ray-ehl |

Jerusalem ---------- dzheh-ROO-suh-lehm
Aaron ------------ EHR-uhn
Levites ------------ LEE-vaits
Lyres ------------- LAI-erz
Cymbals ---------- SIHM-b'lz
*Second Reading*
Immortality ------- ih-mor-TAL-ih-tee

## Assumption
*First Reading*
Diadem ----------- DAI-uh-dehm
*Second Reading*
Sovereignty ------- SAH-vrehn-tee
*Gospel*
Judah ------------- DZHOO-duh
Zechariah -------- zeh-kuh-RAI-uh
Israel ------------- IHZ-ray-ehl
Abraham --------- AY-bruh-ham

## NOVEMBER 1 — ALL SAINTS
*First Reading*
Israelites ---------- IHZ-rih-ehl-aits
Prostrated --------- PRAHS-trayt-ehd
*Gospel*
Righteousness ----- RAI-tshuhs-nehs

## YEAR C

### Season of Advent

#### FIRST SUNDAY OF ADVENT

*First Reading*

| | |
|---|---|
| Israel | IHZ-ray-ehl |
| Judah | DZHOO-duh |
| Jerusalem | dzheh-ROO-suh-lehm |

#### SECOND SUNDAY OF ADVENT

*First Reading*

| | |
|---|---|
| Jerusalem | dzheh-ROO-suh-lehm |
| Israel | IHZ-ray-ehl |
| Mitre | MAI-ter |

*Gospel*

| | |
|---|---|
| Tiberius | tai-BIHR-ih-uhs |
| Caesar | SEE-zer |
| Pontius Pilate | PAHN-shoos PAI-luht |
| Judea | dzhoo-DEE-uh |
| Herod | HEHR-uhd |
| Tetrarch | TEH-trahrk |
| Galilee | GAL-ih-lee |
| Ituraea | ih-TSHOOR-ree-uh |

| | |
|---|---|
| Trachonitis | trak-o-NAI-tihs |
| Lysanias | lai-SAY-nih-uhs |
| Abilene | ab-uh-LEE-nee |
| Annas | AN-uhs |
| Caiaphas | KAY-uh-fuhs |
| Zechariah | zeh-kuh-RAI-uh |
| Isaiah | ai-ZAY-uh |

## THIRD SUNDAY OF ADVENT
*First Reading*

| | |
|---|---|
| Zion | ZAI-uhn |
| Israel | IHZ-ray-ehl |
| Jerusalem | dzheh-ROO-suh-lehm |

## FOURTH SUNDAY OF ADVENT
*First Reading*

| | |
|---|---|
| Bethlehem | BEHTH-leh-hehm |
| Ephrathah | EHF-ruh-thuh |
| Judah | DZHOO-duh |
| Israel | IHZ-ray-ehl |

*Second Reading*

| | |
|---|---|
| Holocausts | HAHL-o-kawsts |

*Gospel*

| | |
|---|---|
| Judah | DZHOO-duh |
| Zechariah | zeh-kuh-RAI-uh |

## YEAR C

### Season of Christmas

#### CHRISTMAS — VIGIL MASS

*First Reading*

| | |
|---|---|
| Zion | ZAI-uhn |
| Jerusalem | dzheh-ROO-suh-lehm |
| Vindication | vihn-dih-KAY-shuhn |
| Diadem | DAI-uh-dehm |
| Espoused | eh-SPAUZD |

*Second Reading*

| | |
|---|---|
| Antioch | AN-tih-ahk |
| Pisidia | pih-SIH-dih-uh |
| Synagogue | SIHN-uh-gahg |
| Israelites | IHZ-rih-ehl-aits |
| Israel | IHZ-ray-ehl |
| Sojourn | SO-dzhern |
| Jesse | DZHEH-see |

*Gospel*

| | |
|---|---|
| Genealogy | dzhee-nee-AH-lo-dzhee |
| Abraham | AY-bruh-ham |
| Isaac | AI-zuhk |
| Jacob | DZHAY-kuhb |
| Judah | DZHOO-duh |
| Perez | PEE-rehz |
| Zerah | ZEE-ruh |
| Tamar | TAY-mer |
| Hezron | HEHZ-ruhn |

| | |
|---|---|
| Ram ------------- | RAM |
| Amminadab ------ | ah-MIHN-uh-dab |
| Nahshon --------- | NAH-shuhn |
| Salmon ----------- | SAL-muhn |
| Boaz------------- | BO-az |
| Rahab ------------ | RAY-hab |
| Obed ------------- | O-behd |
| Jesse ------------- | DZHEH-see |
| Solomon ---------- | SAH-luh-muhn |
| Uriah ------------- | yoo-RAI-uh |
| Rehoboam ------- | ree-ho-BO-am |
| Abijah ------------ | uh-BAI-dzhuh |
| Asaph ------------ | AY-saf |
| Jehoshaphat ------- | dzhee-HAHSH-uh-fat |
| Joram ------------- | DZHO-ram |
| Uzziah ----------- | yoo-ZAI-uh |
| Jotham ----------- | DZHO-thuhm |
| Ahaz ------------- | AY-haz |
| Hezekiah --------- | heh-zeh-KAI-uh |
| Manasseh --------- | man-AS-eh |
| Amos ------------- | AY-muhs |
| Josiah ------------- | dzho-SAI-uh |
| Jechoniah --------- | dzhehk-o-NAI-uh |
| Babylonian ------- | bab-ih-LO-nih-uhn |
| Shealtiel ---------- | shee-AL-tih-ehl |
| Zerubbabel ------- | zeh-RUH-buh-behl |
| Abiud ------------ | uh-BAI-uhd |
| Eliakim ----------- | ee-LAI-uh-kihm |

| | |
|---|---|
| Azor | AY-zawr |
| Zadok | ZAY-dahk |
| Achim | AY-kihm |
| Eliud | ee-LAI-uhd |
| Eleazar | ehl-ee-AY-zer |
| Matthan | MAT-than |
| Emmanuel | eh-MAN-yoo-ehl |

## CHRISTMAS — MIDNIGHT MASS

*First Reading*

| | |
|---|---|
| Midian | MIH-dih-uhn |

*Gospel*

| | |
|---|---|
| Caesar Augustus | SEE-zer uh-GUHS-tuhs |
| Quirinius | kwai-RIHN-ih-uhs |
| Syria | SIHR-ee-uh |
| Galilee | GAL-ih-lee |
| Nazareth | NAZ-uh-rehth |
| Judea | dzhoo-DEE-uh |
| Bethlehem | BEHTH-leh-hehm |
| Betrothed | bee-TRO**TH**D |
| Swaddling | SWAHD-lihng |

## CHRISTMAS — MASS AT DAWN

*First Reading*

| | |
|---|---|
| Zion | ZAI-uhn |

*Gospel*

| | |
|---|---|
| Bethlehem | BEHTH-leh-hehm |

## CHRISTMAS — MASS DURING THE DAY
*First Reading*

| | |
|---|---|
| Zion | ZAI-uhn |
| Jerusalem | dzheh-ROO-suh-lehm |

*Second Reading*

| | |
|---|---|
| Refulgence | ree-FOOL-dzhents |
| Purification | pyoor-ih-fih-KAY-shuhn |

## HOLY FAMILY
*First Reading*

| | |
|---|---|
| Hannah | HAN-uh |
| Samuel | SAM-yoo-uhl |
| Elkanah | ehl-KAY-nuh |
| Nazirite | NAZ-uh-rait |
| Shiloh | SHAI-lo |
| Eli | EE-lai |

*Gospel*

| | |
|---|---|
| Jerusalem | dzheh-ROO-suh-lehm |
| Nazareth | NAZ-uh-rehth |

## JANUARY 1 — SOLEMNITY OF THE BLESSED VIRGIN MARY, THE MOTHER OF GOD
*First Reading*

| | |
|---|---|
| Aaron | EHR-uhn |
| Israelites | IHZ-rih-ehl-aits |

*Second Reading*

| | |
|---|---|
| Abba | AB-uh |

*Gospel*
| | |
|---|---|
| Bethlehem | BEHTH-leh-hehm |
| Circumcision | ser-kuhm-SIHZH-uhn |

## SECOND SUNDAY AFTER CHRISTMAS
*First Reading*
| | |
|---|---|
| Sirach | SAI-rak |
| Zion | ZAI-uhn |

*Second Reading*
| | |
|---|---|
| Ephesians | eh-FEE-zhuhnz |

## THE EPIPHANY OF THE LORD
*First Reading*
| | |
|---|---|
| Jerusalem | dzheh-ROO-suh-lehm |
| Dromedaries | DRAH-muh-dehr-eez |
| Midian | MIH-dih-uhn |
| Ephah | EE-fuh |
| Sheba | SHEE-buh |
| Frankincense | FRANGK-ihn-sehns |

*Second Reading*
| | |
|---|---|
| Stewardship | STOO-erd-shihp |
| Revelation | reh-veh-LAY-shuhn |
| Gentiles | DZHEHN-tailz |
| Coheirs | ko-EHRZ |

*Gospel*
| | |
|---|---|
| Bethlehem | BEHTH-leh-hehm |
| Judea | dzhoo-DEE-uh |
| Herod | HEHR-uhd |

| | |
|---|---|
| Magi ------------- | MAY-dzhai |
| Jerusalem --------- | dzheh-ROO-suh-lehm |
| Judah ------------- | DZHOO-duh |
| Israel ------------- | IHZ-ray-ehl |
| Ascertained ------- | as-er-TAYND |
| Frankincense ----- | FRANGK-ihn-sehns |
| Myrrh ------------ | MER |

## THE BAPTISM OF THE LORD
*First Reading*

| | |
|---|---|
| Isaiah ------------- | ai-ZAY-uh |
| Jerusalem --------- | dzheh-ROO-suh-lehm |
| Zion ------------- | ZAI-uhn |

# YEAR C

## Season of Lent

## ASH WEDNESDAY
*First Reading*

| | |
|---|---|
| Zion ------------- | ZAI-uhn |

*Second Reading*

| | |
|---|---|
| Ambassadors ------ | am-BAS-uh-derz |

*Gospel*

| | |
|---|---|
| Synagogues ------- | SIHN-uh-gahgz |
| Hypocrites ------- | HIHP-uh-krihts |

## FIRST SUNDAY OF LENT

*First Reading*

| | |
|---|---|
| Aramean | ehr-uh-MEE-uhn |

*Gospel*

| | |
|---|---|
| Jerusalem | dzheh-ROO-suh-lehm |

## SECOND SUNDAY OF LENT

*First Reading*

| | |
|---|---|
| Ur | ER |
| Abram | AY-br'm |
| Chaldeans | kal-DEE-uhnz |
| Wadi | WAH-dee |
| Euphrates | yoo-FRAY-teez |

*Gospel*

| | |
|---|---|
| Elijah | ee-LAI-dzhuh |
| Jerusalem | dzheh-ROO-suh-lehm |

## THIRD SUNDAY OF LENT

*First Reading*

| | |
|---|---|
| Jethro | DZHEHTH-ro |
| Midian | MIH-dih-uhn |
| Horeb | HAWR-ehb |
| Isaac | AI-zuhk |
| Abraham | AY-bruh-ham |
| Israelites | IHZ-rih-ehl-aits |

*Gospel*

| | |
|---|---|
| Galileans | gal-ih-LEE-uhnz |
| Siloam | sih-LO-uhm |
| Jerusalem | dzheh-ROO-suh-lehm |

## FOURTH SUNDAY OF LENT
*First Reading*

| | |
|---|---|
| Joshua | DZHAH-shoo-uh |
| Israelites | IHZ-rih-ehl-aits |
| Gilgal | GIHL-gal |
| Jericho | DZHEHR-ih-ko |
| Manna | MAN-uh |
| Canaan | KAY-nuhn |

*Gospel*

| | |
|---|---|
| Pharisees | FEHR-ih-seez |

## FIFTH SUNDAY OF LENT
*Gospel*

| | |
|---|---|
| Pharisees | FEHR-ih-seez |

## PALM SUNDAY OF THE LORD'S PASSION
*Gospel at the Procession with Palms*

| | |
|---|---|
| Jerusalem | dzheh-ROO-suh-lehm |
| Bethphage | BEHTH-fuh-dzhee |
| Bethany | BEHTH-uh-nee |
| Pharisees | FEHR-ih-seez |

*Gospel (Passion)*

| | |
|---|---|
| Gentiles | DZHEHN-tailz |
| Israel | IHZ-ray-ehl |
| Judas | DZHOO-duhs |
| Galilean | gal-ih-LEE-uhn |
| Prophesy | PRAH-feh-sai |
| Sanhedrin | san-HEE-drihn |
| Judea | dzhoo-DEE-uh |

| | |
|---|---|
| Galilee | GAL-ih-lee |
| Jerusalem | dzheh-ROO-suh-lehm |
| Barabbas | buh-RAB-uhs |
| Cyrenian | sai-REE-nih-uhn |
| Centurion | sehn-TSHOOR-ee-uhn |
| Arimathea | ehr-uh-muh-THEE-uh |

## YEAR C

### Easter Triduum and Season of Easter

#### HOLY THURSDAY
*First Reading*

| | |
|---|---|
| Israel | IHZ-ray-ehl |
| Procuring | pro-KYOOR-ihng |

*Gospel*

| | |
|---|---|
| Passover | PAS-o-ver |
| Judas | DZHOO-duhs |
| Iscariot | ihs-KEHR-ee-uht |

#### GOOD FRIDAY
*First Reading*

| | |
|---|---|
| Chastisement | tshas-TAIZ-mehnt |
| Smitten | SMIHT'n |

*Second Reading*
    Supplications ----- suhp-lih-KAY-shuhnz
*Gospel (Passion)*
    Kidron ----------- KIHD-ruhn
    Judas ------------- DZHOO-duhs
    Pharisees --------- FEHR-ih-seez
    Nazarene --------- naz-uh-REEN
    Malchus ---------- MAL-kuhs
    Annas ------------ AN-uhs
    Caiaphas --------- KAY-uh-fuhs
    Synagogue -------- SIHN-uh-gahg
    Praetorium ------- pray-TAWR-ih-uhm
    Passover ---------- PAS-o-ver
    Pilate ------------- PAI-luht
    Barabbas ---------- buh-RAB-uhs
    Caesar ------------ SEE-zer
    Gabbatha --------- GAB-uh-thuh
    Golgotha --------- GAHL-guh-thuh
    Clopas ------------ KLO-pas
    Magdala ---------- MAG-duh-luh
    Hyssop ----------- HIH-suhp
    Arimathea -------- ehr-uh-muh-THEE-uh
    Nicodemus ------- nih-ko-DEE-muhs
    Myrrh ------------ MER
    Aloes ------------- AL-oz

**EASTER VIGIL**

*First Reading*

| | |
|---|---|
| Abyss | uh-BIHS |
| Luminaries | LOO-mihn-ehr-eez |

*Second Reading*

| | |
|---|---|
| Abraham | AY-bruh-ham |
| Isaac | AI-zuhk |
| Moriah | maw-RAI-uh |
| Holocaust | HAHL-o-kawst |
| Yahweh-Yireh | YAH-weh-yer-AY |

*Third Reading*

| | |
|---|---|
| Israelites | IHZ-rih-ehl-aits |
| Pharaoh | FEHR-o |
| Charioteers | tsher-ih-uh-TEERS |
| Israel | IHZ-ray-ehl |

*Fourth Reading*

| | |
|---|---|
| Israel | IHZ-ray-ehl |
| Noah | NO-uh |
| Carnelians | kahr-NEEL-yuhnz |
| Sapphires | SAF-fai-erz |
| Carbuncles | KAHR-buhng-k'lz |

*Fifth Reading*

| | |
|---|---|
| Israel | IHZ-ray-ehl |

*Sixth Reading*

| | |
|---|---|
| Israel | IHZ-ray-ehl |
| Jacob | DZHAY-kuhb |
| Netherworld | NEH**TH**-er-werld |

*Seventh Reading*
    Profaned ----------- pro-FAYND
    Israel ------------- IHZ-ray-ehl
*Gospel*
    Galilee ------------ GAL-ih-lee
    Magdalene -------- MAG-duh-lehn
    Joanna ------------ dzho-AN-uh

## EASTER SUNDAY
*First Reading*
    Judea ------------- dzhoo-DEE-uh
    Galilee ------------ GAL-ih-lee
    Nazareth --------- NAZ-uh-rehth
    Jerusalem --------- dzheh-ROO-suh-lehm
*Second Reading*
    Paschal ----------- PAS-k'l
*Gospel*
    Magdala ----------- MAG-duh-luh
*Gospel (used at Masses later in the day)*
    Jerusalem --------- dzheh-ROO-suh-lehm
    Emmaus ----------- eh-MAY-uhs
    Cleopas ----------- KLEE-o-pas
    Nazarene --------- naz-uh-REEN
    Israel ------------- IHZ-ray-ehl

## SECOND SUNDAY OF EASTER
*First Reading*
    Solomon --------- SAH-luh-muhn
    Portico ----------- PAWR-tih-ko

Jerusalem ---------- dzheh-ROO-suh-lehm
*Second Reading*
    Patmos ------------ PAT-mos
*Gospel*
    Didymus ---------- DIHD-ih-m**oo**s

## THIRD SUNDAY OF EASTER
*First Reading*
    Sanhedrin -------- san-HEE-drihn
    Jerusalem ---------- dzheh-ROO-suh-lehm
    Israel ------------- IHZ-ray-ehl
*Gospel*
    Tiberius ----------- tai-BIHR-ih-uhs
    Didymus ---------- DIHD-ih-m**oo**s
    Nathanael --------- nuh-THAN-ay-ehl
    Cana ------------- KAY-nuh
    Galilee ------------ GAL-ih-lee
    Zebedee ----------- ZEH-beh-dee

## FOURTH SUNDAY OF EASTER
*First Reading*
    Barnabas ----------- BAHR-nuh-buhs
    Perga ------------- PER-guh
    Antioch ----------- AN-tih-ahk
    Pisidia ------------ pih-SIH-dih-uh
    Synagogue -------- SIHN-uh-gahg
    Judaism ----------- DZHOO-duh-ihz'm
    Gentiles ---------- DZHEHN-tailz

## FIFTH SUNDAY OF EASTER
*First Reading*

| | |
|---|---|
| Barnabas | BAHR-nuh-buhs |
| Lystra | LIHS-truh |
| Iconium | ai-KO-nih-uhm |
| Antioch | AN-tih-ahk |
| Pisidia | pih-SIH-dih-uh |
| Pamphylia | pam-FIHL-ih-uh |
| Perga | PER-guh |
| Attalia | at-TAH-lee-uh |
| Gentiles | DZHEHN-tailz |

*Second Reading*

| | |
|---|---|
| Jerusalem | dzheh-ROO-suh-lehm |

*Gospel*

| | |
|---|---|
| Judas | DZHOO-duhs |

## SIXTH SUNDAY OF EASTER
*First Reading*

| | |
|---|---|
| Judea | dzhoo-DEE-uh |
| Circumcised | ser-kuhm-SAIZD |
| Mosaic | mo-ZAY-ihk |
| Barnabas | BAHR-nuh-buhs |
| Jerusalem | dzheh-ROO-suh-lehm |
| Antioch | AN-tih-ahk |
| Judas | DZHOO-duhs |
| Barsabbas | BAHR-suh-buhs |
| Silas | SAI-luhs |
| Syria | SIHR-ee-uh |

    Cilicia ------------- sih-LIHSH-ee-uh
*Second Reading*
    Jerusalem ---------- dzheh-ROO-suh-lehm
    Israelites ---------- IHZ-rih-ehl-aits

## THE ASCENSION OF THE LORD
*First Reading*
    Theophilus -------- thee-AH-fih-luhs
    Jerusalem ---------- dzheh-ROO-suh-lehm
    Israel ------------- IHZ-ray-ehl
    Judea -------------- dzhoo-DEE-uh
    Samaria ------------ suh-MEHR-ih-uh
    Galilee ------------ GAL-ih-lee
*Second Reading*
    Sanctuary ---------- SANG-tshoo-ehr-ee
*Gospel*
    Bethany ----------- BEHTH-uh-nee
    Jerusalem ---------- dzheh-ROO-suh-lehm

## SEVENTH SUNDAY OF EASTER
*Second Reading*
    Recompense ----- REH-kuhm-pehns
    Alpha ------------- AHL-fuh
    Omega ----------- o-MAY-guh

## PENTECOST VIGIL
*First Reading*
    Shinar ------------- SHAI-nahr

| | |
|---|---|
| Bitumen ----------- | bih-TYOO-m'n |
| Babel ------------- | BAY-b'l |
| Israelites ----------- | IHZ-rih-ehl-aits |
| Sinai -------------- | SAI-nai |
| Ezekiel ----------- | eh-ZEE-kee-'l |
| Sinews ------------ | SIHN-yooz |
| Prophesy --------- | PRAH-feh-sai |
| Israel ------------- | IHZ-ray-ehl |
| Zion -------------- | ZAI-uhn |
| Jerusalem --------- | dzheh-ROO-suh-lehm |

## PENTECOST
### First Reading

| | |
|---|---|
| Jerusalem --------- | dzheh-ROO-suh-lehm |
| Galileans ----------- | gal-ih-LEE-uhnz |
| Parthians --------- | PAHR-thee-uhnz |
| Medes ------------- | MEEDZ |
| Elamites ----------- | EE-luh-maits |
| Mesopotamia ----- | mehs-uh-po-TAY-mih-uh |
| Judea -------------- | dzhoo-DEE-uh |
| Cappadocia ------- | kap-uh-DO-shee-uh |
| Pontus ------------- | PAHN-tuhs |
| Phrygia ----------- | FRIH-dzhih-uh |
| Pamphylia -------- | pam-FIHL-ih-uh |
| Libya -------------- | LIH-bih-uh |
| Cyrene ----------- | sai-REE-nee |
| Judaism ----------- | DZHOO-duh-ihz'm |

Cretans ------------ KREE-tihnz
*Second Reading*
    Abba -------------- AB-uh

## YEAR C
### Ordinary Time

### SECOND SUNDAY IN ORDINARY TIME
*First Reading*
    Zion -------------- ZAI-uhn
    Jerusalem ---------- dzheh-ROO-suh-lehm
    Diadem ------------ DAI-uh-dehm
*Gospel*
    Cana -------------- KAY-nuh
    Galilee ------------ GAL-ih-lee

### THIRD SUNDAY IN ORDINARY TIME
*First Reading*
    Ezra --------------- EHZ-ruh
    Nehemiah --------- nee-hee-MAI-uh
    Levites ------------ LEE-vaits
*Gospel*
    Theophilus ------- thee-AH-fih-luhs
    Galilee ------------ GAL-ih-lee
    Synagogues ------- SIHN-uh-gahgz
    Nazareth --------- NAZ-uh-rehth
    Isaiah ------------- ai-ZAY-uh

## FOURTH SUNDAY IN ORDINARY TIME
*First Reading*

| | |
|---|---|
| Judah | DZHOO-duh |

*Second Reading*

| | |
|---|---|
| Cymbal | SIHM-b'l |
| Prophesy | PRAH-feh-sai |

*Gospel*

| | |
|---|---|
| Synagogue | SIHN-uh-gahg |
| Capernaum | kuh-PER-nay-uhm |
| Israel | IHZ-ray-ehl |
| Elijah | ee-LAI-dzhuh |
| Zarephath | ZEHR-ee-fath |
| Sidon | SAI-duhn |
| Elisha | ee-LAI-shuh |
| Naaman | NAY-uh-muhn |
| Syrian | SIHR-ee-uhn |

## FIFTH SUNDAY IN ORDINARY TIME
*First Reading*

| | |
|---|---|
| Uzziah | yoo-ZAI-uh |
| Seraphim | SEHR-uh-fihm |

*Second Reading*

| | |
|---|---|
| Cephas | SEE-fuhs |

*Gospel*

| | |
|---|---|
| Gennesaret | gehn-NEHS-uh-reht |
| Zebedee | ZEH-beh-dee |

## SIXTH SUNDAY IN ORDINARY TIME
*Gospel*

| | |
|---|---|
| Judea | dzhoo-DEE-uh |
| Jerusalem | dzheh-ROO-suh-lehm |
| Tyre | TAI-er |
| Sidon | SAI-duhn |

## SEVENTH SUNDAY IN ORDINARY TIME
*First Reading*

| | |
|---|---|
| Ziph | ZIHF |
| Israel | IHZ-ray-ehl |
| Abishai | uh-BIHSH-ay-ai |
| Ner | NER |

## EIGHTH SUNDAY IN ORDINARY TIME
*First Reading*

| | |
|---|---|
| Sieve | SIHV |

## NINTH SUNDAY IN ORDINARY TIME
*First Reading*

| | |
|---|---|
| Israel | IHZ-ray-ehl |
| Solomon | SAH-luh-muhn |

*Second Reading*

| | |
|---|---|
| Galatia | guh-LAY-shih-uh |

*Gospel*

| | |
|---|---|
| Israel | IHZ-ray-ehl |

## TENTH SUNDAY IN ORDINARY TIME
*First Reading*

| | |
|---|---|
| Elijah | ee-LAI-dzhuh |

| | |
|---|---|
| Zarephath | ZEHR-ee-fath |
| Sidon | SAI-duhn |

*Second Reading*

| | |
|---|---|
| Judaism | DZHOO-duh-ihz'm |
| Gentiles | DZHEHN-tailz |
| Cephas | SEE-fuhs |

*Gospel*

| | |
|---|---|
| Nain | NAY-ihn |
| Judea | dzhoo-DEE-uh |

## ELEVENTH SUNDAY IN ORDINARY TIME

*First Reading*

| | |
|---|---|
| Nathan | NAY-thuhn |
| Israel | IHZ-ray-ehl |
| Uriah | yoo-RAI-uh |
| Hittite | HIH-tait |
| Ammonites | AM-uh-naits |

*Gospel*

| | |
|---|---|
| Magdalene | MAG-duh-lehn |
| Chuza | KOO-zuh |

## TWELFTH SUNDAY IN ORDINARY TIME

*First Reading*

| | |
|---|---|
| Hadadrimmon | hay-dad-RIHM-uhn |
| Megiddo | mee-GIH-do |

*Gospel*

| | |
|---|---|
| Elijah | ee-LAI-dzhuh |

## THIRTEENTH SUNDAY IN ORDINARY TIME
*First Reading*

| | |
|---|---|
| Elijah | ee-LAI-dzhuh |
| Elisha | ee-LAI-shuh |
| Shaphat | SHAY-fat |
| Abelmeholah | AY-b'l-mee-HO-luh |

*Gospel*

| | |
|---|---|
| Jerusalem | dzheh-ROO-suh-lehm |
| Samaritan | suh-MEHR-ih-tuhn |

## FOURTEENTH SUNDAY IN ORDINARY TIME
*First Reading*

| | |
|---|---|
| Jerusalem | dzheh-ROO-suh-lehm |

*Second Reading*

| | |
|---|---|
| Circumcision | ser-kuhm-SIHZH-uhn |
| Israel | IHZ-ray-ehl |

*Gospel*

| | |
|---|---|
| Sodom | SAH-duhm |

## FIFTEENTH SUNDAY IN ORDINARY TIME
*Second Reading*

| | |
|---|---|
| Principalities | prihn-sih-PAL-uh-teez |

*Gospel*

| | |
|---|---|
| Jerusalem | dzheh-ROO-suh-lehm |
| Jericho | DZHEHR-ih-ko |
| Levite | LEE-vait |
| Samaritan | suh-MEHR-ih-tuhn |

## SIXTEENTH SUNDAY IN ORDINARY TIME

*First Reading*

Abraham ---------- AY-bruh-ham

Mamre ----------- MAM-ree

*Second Reading*

Gentiles ---------- DZHEHN-tailz

## SEVENTEENTH SUNDAY IN ORDINARY TIME

*First Reading*

Sodom ----------- SAH-duhm

Gomorrah -------- guh-MAWR-uh

Abraham ---------- AY-bruh-ham

*Second Reading*

Transgressions ---- trans-GREHSH-uhnzs

Uncircumcision -- uhn-ser-kuhm-
SIHZH-uhn

## EIGHTEENTH SUNDAY IN ORDINARY TIME

*First Reading*

Qoheleth ---------- ko-HEHL-ehth

*Second Reading*

Circumcision ----- ser-kuhm-SIHZH-uhn

Uncircumcision -- uhn-ser-kuhm-
SIHZH-uhn

Scythian ---------- SIH-thee-uhn

*Gospel*

Arbitrator --------- AHR-bih-tray-ter

**NINETEENTH SUNDAY IN ORDINARY TIME**
*Second Reading*

| | |
|---|---|
| Abraham | AY-bruh-ham |
| Isaac | AI-zuhk |

**TWENTIETH SUNDAY IN ORDINARY TIME**
*First Reading*

| | |
|---|---|
| Jeremiah | dzhehr-eh-MAI-uh |
| Zedekiah | zeh-dee-KAI-uh |
| Malchiah | mal-KAI-uh |
| Ebed-Melech | EE-behd-MEE-lehk |
| Cushite | CUHSH-ait |

**TWENTY-FIRST SUNDAY IN ORDINARY TIME**
*First Reading*

| | |
|---|---|
| Tarshish | TAHR-shihsh |
| Put | PUHT |
| Lud | LUHD |
| Mosoch | MAH-sahk |
| Tubal | TYOO-b'l |
| Javan | DZHAY-van |
| Dromedaries | DRAH-muh-dehr-eez |
| Jerusalem | dzheh-ROO-suh-lehm |
| Israelites | IHZ-rih-ehl-aits |
| Levites | LEE-vaits |

*Gospel*

| | |
|---|---|
| Jerusalem | dzheh-ROO-suh-lehm |
| Abraham | AY-bruh-ham |
| Isaac | AI-zuhk |

## TWENTY-SECOND SUNDAY IN ORDINARY TIME

*Second Reading*

Zion ------------- ZAI-uhn
Jerusalem --------- dzheh-ROO-suh-lehm
Abel -------------- AY-b'l

*Gospel*

Pharisees --------- FEHR-ih-seez

## TWENTY-THIRD SUNDAY IN ORDINARY TIME

*Second Reading*

Onesimus--------- o-NEH-sih-muhs

## TWENTY-FOURTH SUNDAY IN ORDINARY TIME

*First Reading*

Israel ------------- IHZ-ray-ehl
Isaac -------------- AI-zuhk
Abraham --------- AY-bruh-ham

*Gospel*

Pharisees --------- FEHR-ih-seez

## TWENTY-FIFTH SUNDAY IN ORDINARY TIME

*First Reading*

Ephah ------------- EE-fuh
Shekel ------------- SHEHK-uhl

*Second Reading*

Gentiles ---------- DZHEHN-tailz

*Gospel*
- Kors -------------- KORZ
- Mammon --------- MAM-uhn

## TWENTY-SIXTH SUNDAY IN ORDINARY TIME
*First Reading*
- Zion -------------- ZAI-uhn

*Second Reading*
- Pontius Pilate ----- PAHN-shoos PAI-luht

*Gospel*
- Pharisees --------- FEHR-ih-seez
- Lazarus ----------- LAZ-er-uhs
- Abraham --------- AY-bruh-ham
- Chasm ------------ KAZ'm

## TWENTY-SEVENTH SUNDAY IN ORDINARY TIME
*First Reading*
- Habakkuk --------- huh-BAK-uhk

## TWENTY-EIGHTH SUNDAY IN ORDINARY TIME
*First Reading*
- Naaman ----------- NAY-uh-muhn
- Elisha ------------- ee-LAI-shuh
- Israel ------------- IHZ-ray-ehl
- Holocaust -------- HAHL-o-kawst

*Gospel*
- Jerusalem --------- dzheh-ROO-suh-lehm

| | |
|---|---|
| Samaria ----------- | suh-MEHR-ih-uh |
| Galilee ------------ | GAL-ih-lee |
| Samaritan --------- | suh-MEHR-ih-tuhn |

## TWENTY-NINTH SUNDAY IN ORDINARY TIME
*First Reading*

| | |
|---|---|
| Amalek ----------- | AM-uh-lehk |
| Israel ------------- | IHZ-ray-ehl |
| Joshua ------------ | DZHAH-shoo-uh |
| Aaron ------------ | EHR-uhn |
| Hur -------------- | HER |

## THIRTIETH SUNDAY IN ORDINARY TIME
*Second Reading*

| | |
|---|---|
| Gentiles ---------- | DZHEHN-tailz |

*Gospel*

| | |
|---|---|
| Pharisee ---------- | FEHR-ih-see |

## THIRTY-FIRST SUNDAY IN ORDINARY TIME
*Gospel*

| | |
|---|---|
| Jericho ----------- | DZHEHR-ih-ko |
| Zacchaeus -------- | zak-KEE-uhs |
| Abraham --------- | AY-bruh-ham |

## THIRTY-SECOND SUNDAY IN ORDINARY TIME
*Gospel*

| | |
|---|---|
| Sadducees -------- | SAD-dzhoo-seez |

Abraham ---------- AY-bruh-ham
Isaac -------------- AI-zuhk

## THIRTY-THIRD SUNDAY IN ORDINARY TIME
*First Reading*
Malachi------------ MAL-uh-kai

## CHRIST THE KING
*First Reading*
Israel -------------- IHZ-ray-ehl
Hebron ------------ HEE-bruhn
Israelites ----------- IHZ-rih-ehl-aits

## YEAR C

### Solemnities of the Lord
### During Ordinary Time

## THE SOLEMNITY OF THE MOST HOLY TRINITY
*First Reading*
Prodigies ---------- PRAH-dih-dzheez

## THE SOLEMNITY OF THE MOST HOLY BODY AND BLOOD OF CHRIST
*First Reading*
Melchizedek ------ mehl-KIHZ-eh-dehk

Salem -------------- SAY-lehm
Abram ------------ AY-br'm

## YEAR C

### Other Solemnities

### DECEMBER 8 — THE IMMACULATE CONCEPTION OF THE BLESSED VIRGIN MARY

*First Reading*
    Enmity ------------ EHN-mih-tee
*Gospel*
    Gabriel ------------ GAY-bree-'l
    Galilee ------------- GAL-ih-lee
    Nazareth --------- NAZ-uh-rehth
    Jacob ------------- DZHAY-kuhb

### AUGUST 15 — THE ASSUMPTION OF THE BLESSED VIRGIN MARY

### Assumption Vigil

*First Reading*
    Israel -------------- IHZ-ray-ehl
    Jerusalem --------- dzheh-ROO-suh-lehm
    Aaron ------------ EHR-uhn
    Levites ------------ LEE-vaits

Lyres -------------- LAI-erz
Cymbals ----------- SIHM-b'lz
*Second Reading*
Immortality ------- ih-mor-TAL-ih-tee

## Assumption
*First Reading*
Diadem ------------ DAI-uh-dehm
*Second Reading*
Sovereignty ------- SAH-vrehn-tee
*Gospel*
Judah -------------- DZHOO-duh
Zechariah --------- zeh-kuh-RAI-uh
Israel -------------- IHZ-ray-ehl
Abraham ---------- AY-bruh-ham

## November 1 — All Saints
*First Reading*
Israelites ----------- IHZ-rih-ehl-aits
Prostrated --------- PRAHS-trayt-ehd
*Gospel*
Righteousness ---- RAI-tshuhs-nehs

# Alphabetical List of Words

| A | |
|---|---|
| Aaron | EHR-uhn |
| Abana | AB-uh-nuh |
| Abba | AB-uh |
| Abednego | uh-BEHD-nee-go |
| Abel | AY-b'l |
| Abel-Keramin | AY-b'l-KEHR-uh-mihn |
| Abelmeholah | AY-b'l-mee-HO-luh |
| Abiathar | uh-BAI-uh-ther |
| Abiel | AY-bee-ehl |
| Abiezrite | ay-bai-EHZ-rait |
| Abijah | uh-BAI-dzhuh |
| Abilene | ab-uh-LEE-nee |
| Abimelech | uh-BIHM-uh-lehk |
| Abinadab | uh-BIHN-uh-dab |
| Abishai | uh-BIHSH-ay-ai |
| Abiud | uh-BAI-uhd |
| Abraham | AY-bruh-ham |
| Abram | AY-br'm |
| Absalom | AB-suh-luhm |
| Abyss | uh-BIHS |

| | |
|---|---|
| Acacia | uh-KAY-shuh |
| Achaia | uh-KAY-yuh |
| Achbor | AK-bawr |
| Achilleus | uh-KIHL-yoos |
| Achim | AY-kihm |
| Acquittal | uh-KWIHT'l |
| Admonish | ad-MAH-nihsh |
| Aeneas | uh-NEE-uhs |
| Agabus | AG-uh-buhs |
| Agag | AY-gag |
| Agatha | AG-uh-thuh |
| Agrippa | uh-GRIH-puh |
| Ahab | AY-hab |
| Ahaz | AY-haz |
| Ahaziah | ay-haz-AI-uh |
| Ahijah | uh-HAI-dzhuh |
| Ahikam | uh-HAI-kam |
| Ahiqar | ah-hee-KAR |
| Ai | AY-ee |
| Alabaster | al-uh-BAS-ter |
| Alacoque | AL-uh-kok |
| Alexandria | al-ehg-ZAN-dree-uh |
| Alleluia | ah-lay-LOO-yuh |
| Aloes | AL-oz |
| Aloysius | al-o-IHSH-uhs |
| Alpha | AHL-fuh |
| Alphaeus | AL-fee-uhs |

| | |
|---|---|
| Alphonsus | al-FAHN-zoos |
| Ambassadors | am-BAS-uh-derz |
| Amalek | AM-uh-lehk |
| Amalekites | AM-uh-luh-kaits |
| Amaziah | am-uh-ZAI-uh |
| Amen | ah-MEHN |
| Amittai | uh-MIH-tai |
| Amminadab | ah-MIHN-uh-dab |
| Ammonite | AM-uh-nait |
| Ammonites | AM-uh-naits |
| Amorite | AM-uh-rait |
| Amorites | AM-uh-raits |
| Amos | AY-muhs |
| Amoz | AY-muhz |
| Ampliatus | am-plee-AY-tuhs |
| Anakim | AN-uh-kihm |
| Ananias | an-uh-NAI-uhs |
| Anathoth | AN-uh-thahth |
| Andronicus | an-draw-NAI-kuhs |
| Angela Merici | AN-dzheh-luh meh-REE-tshee |
| Annas | AN-uhs |
| Anselm | AN-sehlm |
| Ansgar | ANS-gahr |
| Antichrist | AN-tih-kraist |
| Antioch | AN-tih-ahk |
| Antiochus | an-TAI-uh-kuhs |

| | |
|---|---|
| Aphek | AY-fehk |
| Aphiah | uh-FAI-uh |
| Apollos | uh-PAH-luhs |
| Apostasy | uh-PAHS-tuh-see |
| Appius | AP-ee-uhs |
| Aquila | uh-KWIHL-uh |
| Aquinas | uh-KWAI-nuhs |
| Arab | EHR-uhb |
| Arabah | EHR-uh-buh |
| Aram | AY-ram |
| Aramean | ehr-uh-MEE-uhn |
| Araunah | uh-RAW-nuh |
| Arbitrator | AHR-bih-tray-ter |
| Archangel | AHRK-ayn-dzhul |
| Archelaus | ahr-kee-LAY-uhs |
| Areopagus | ehr-ee-AH-puh-guhs |
| Arimathea | ehr-uh-muh-THEE-uh |
| Aroer | uh-RO-er |
| Artaxerxes | ahr-tak-SERK-seez |
| Asa | AY-suh |
| Asaph | AY-saf |
| Ascertained | as-er-TAYND |
| Asher | ASH-er |
| Ashpenaz | ASH-pee-naz |
| Ashtaroth | ASH-tahr-awth |
| Asmodeus | az-mo-DEE-uhs |
| Aspens | AS-pehnz |

| | |
|---|---|
| Asser | AS-er |
| Assisi | uh-SEE-zee |
| Assyria | a-SIHR-ee-uh |
| Astarte | as-TAHR-tee |
| Athalia | ath-uh-LAI-uh |
| Athanasius | ath-uh-NAY-shuhs |
| Attalia | at-TAH-lee-uh |
| Augustine | uh-GUHS-tihn |
| Aven | AY-v'n |
| Avila | AH-vih-luh |
| Azariah | az-uh-RAI-uh |
| Azor | AY-zawr |
| Azotus | uh-ZO-toos |
| Azzur | AZ-er |

---

## B

| | |
|---|---|
| Baal | BAY-uhl |
| Baal-Shalishah | BAY-uhl-shuh-LAI-shuh |
| Baal-Zephon | BAY-uhl-ZEE-fuhn |
| Baasha | BAY-uh-shuh |
| Babel | BAY-b'l |
| Babylon | BAB-ih-luhn |
| Babylonian | bab-ih-LO-nih-uhn |
| Bahurim | bah-HOOR-ihm |
| Balaam | BAY-l'm |

| | |
|---|---|
| Balak | BAY-lak |
| Balamon | BAL-uh-muhn |
| Baptize | bap-TAIZ |
| Barabbas | buh-RAB-uhs |
| Barak | BEHR-ak |
| Barnabas | BAHR-nuh-buhs |
| Barsabbas | BAHR-suh-buhs |
| Bartholomew | bar-THAHL-uh-myoo |
| Bartimaeus | bar-tih-MEE-uhs |
| Baruch | BEHR-*ook* |
| Bashan | BAY-shan |
| Bathsheba | bath-SHEE-buh |
| Bdellium | DEHL-y*oo*m |
| Becket | BEHK-eht |
| Becorath | bee-KO-rath |
| Bede | BEED |
| Beelzebul | bee-EHL-zee-buhl |
| Beer-Lahairoi | BEE-er-luh-HAI-roi |
| Beer-Sheba | BEE-er-SHEE-buh |
| Bellarmine | BEHL-er-mihn |
| Belshazzar | behl-SHAZ-er |
| Benedict | BEHN-eh-dihkt |
| Benjaminite | BEHN-dzhuh-mihn-ait |
| Beor | BEE-awr |
| Bethany | BEHTH-uh-nee |
| Bethel | BETH'l |
| Bethesda | beh-THEHZ-duh |

| | |
|---|---|
| Bethlehem | BEHTH-leh-hehm |
| Beth-Millo | BEHTH-mihl-o |
| Beth-Peor | behth-PEE-awr |
| Bethphage | BEHTH-fuh-dzhee |
| Bethsaida | behth-SAY-ih-duh |
| Bethulia | bee-THOO-lee-uh |
| Beth-Zur | behth-ZER |
| Betrothed | bee-TRO*TH*D |
| Bithynia | bih-THIHN-ih-uh |
| Bitumen | bih-TYOO-m'n |
| Blase | BLAYZ |
| Blasphemed | blas-FEEMD |
| Blasphemy | BLAS-fuh-mee |
| Boanerges | bo-uh-NER-dzheez |
| Boaz | BO-az |
| Bonaventure | bah-nuh-VEHN-tsher |
| Booths (Feast of) | BOO*TH*S |
| Borromeo | baw-ro-MAY-o |
| Bosco | BAHS-ko |
| Brazier | BRAY-zher |
| Bridget | BRIH-dzhet |
| Brigand | BRIH-g'nd |
| Brindisi | brihn-DEE-zee |
| Bullock | B**OO**L-uhk |

## C

| | |
|---|---|
| Caesar ----------- | SEE-zer |
| Caesar Augustus - | SEE-zer uh-GUHS-tuhs |
| Caesarea --------- | sehz-er-EE-uh |
| Caesarea Philippi- | sehz-er-EE-uh fih-LIH-pai |
| Caiaphas --------- | KAY-uh-fuhs |
| Cain ------------- | KAYN |
| Cajetan ---------- | KADZH-uh-tuhn |
| Calasanz (Joseph)-- | KAL-uh-sahnz |
| Caleb ------------ | KAY-lehb |
| Callistus --------- | cuh-LIHS-tuhs |
| Camillus --------- | cuh-MIHL-uhs |
| de Lellis ------- | deh LEHL-ihs |
| Cana ------------- | KAY-nuh |
| Canaan ---------- | KAY-nuhn |
| Canaanite -------- | KAY-nuh-nait |
| Candace --------- | kan-DAY-see |
| Canisius --------- | kuh-NEE-shuhs |
| Capernaum ------ | kuh-PER-nay-uhm |
| Capistrano ------- | kah-pih-STRAH-no |
| Cappadocia ------ | kap-uh-DO-shee-uh |
| Carbuncles------- | KAHR-buhng-k'lz |
| Carians ---------- | KAY-rih-uhnz |
| Carmel ---------- | KAHR-muhl |

| | |
|---|---|
| Carnelian --------- | kahr-NEEL-yuhn |
| Carnelians ------- | kahr-NEEL-yuhnz |
| Carpus ----------- | KAHR-puhs |
| Casimir ----------- | KAZ-ih-mer |
| Cecilia ----------- | suh-SEEL-yuh |
| Cenacle----------- | SEHN-uh-k'l |
| Cenchreae ------- | SEHN-kree-ay |
| Census----------- | SEHN-suhs |
| Centurion ------- | sehn-TSHOOR-ee-uhn |
| Cephas ----------- | SEE-fuhs |
| Chaldeans ------- | kal-DEE-uhnz |
| Charioteers ------ | tsher-ih-uh-TEERS |
| Chasm ----------- | KAZ'm |
| Chastisement ---- | tshas-TAIZ-mehnt |
| Chebar ----------- | KEE-bahr |
| Chemosh --------- | KEE-mahsh |
| Cherubim -------- | TSHEHR-oo-bihm |
| Chilion ----------- | KIHL-ee-ahn |
| Chislev ----------- | KIHS-lehv |
| Chloe ----------- | KLO-ee |
| Chorazin -------- | kor-AY-zihn |
| Chrism ----------- | KRIH-s'm |
| Chronicles ------- | KRAH-nih-k'lz |
| Chrysologus ----- | krih-SAHL-uh-guhs |
| Chrysostom ----- | KRIHS-uhs-tuhm |
| Chuza ----------- | KOO-zuh |
| Cilicia ----------- | sih-LIHSH-ee-uh |

| | |
|---|---|
| Circumcised ----- | ser-kuhm-SAIZD |
| Circumcision ---- | ser-kuhm-SIHZH-uhn |
| Claret (bishop) --- | KLEHR-eht |
| Claudius ---------- | KLAW-dee-*oo*s |
| Clemency ------- | KLEHM-uhn-see |
| Cleopas ----------- | KLEE-o-pas |
| Clopas ------------ | KLO-pas |
| Coheirs ----------- | ko-EHRZ |
| Colossae ---------- | ko-LAH-see |
| Colossians ------- | kuh-LAH-shihnz |
| Columban ------- | kuh-LUHM-b'n |
| Condemnation -- | kahn-dehm-NAY-shuhn |
| Consecrated ----- | KAHN-seh-kray-tehd |
| Coriander ------- | kawr-ee-AN-der |
| Corinth ---------- | KAWR-ihnth |
| Corinthians ------ | kawr-IHN-thee-uhnz |
| Cornelius -------- | kawr-NEE-lee-uhs |
| Cosmas ----------- | KAHZ-muhs |
| Counselor ------- | KAUN-seh-ler |
| Covenant -------- | KUH-veh-n'nt |
| Crescens --------- | KREH-sihns |
| Cretans ---------- | KREE-tihnz |
| Crete ------------- | KREET |
| Crispus ----------- | KRIHS-puhs |
| Cushite ----------- | CUHSH-ait |
| Cymbal ----------- | SIHM-b'l |
| Cymbals ---------- | SIHM-b'lz |

| | |
|---|---|
| Cyprian | SIH-pree-'n |
| Cyprus | SAI-pruhs |
| Cyrene | sai-REE-nee |
| Cyrenean | sai-REE-nee-uhn |
| Cyrenian | sai-REE-nih-uhn |
| Cyrus | SAI-ruhs |

## D

| | |
|---|---|
| Dalmatia | dal-MAY-shih-uh |
| Damaris | DAM-uh-rihs |
| Damascene | DAM-uh-seen |
| Damascus | duh-MAS-kuhs |
| Danites | DAN-aits |
| Darius | duh-RAI-uhs |
| Decapolis | dee-KAP-o-lihs |
| de Chantal | deh shahn-TAHL |
| Demas | DEE-mas |
| de Pazzi | deh PAHT-see |
| Derbe | DER-bee |
| Deuteronomy | dyoo-ter-AH-nuh-mee |
| Diadem | DAI-uh-dehm |
| Didymus | DIHD-ih-moos |
| Dionysius | dai-o-NIHSH-ih-uhs |
| Disciples | dih-SAI-p'lz |
| Dorcas | DAWR-kuhs |
| Dothan | DO-thuhn |

Dromedaries ----- DRAH-muh-dehr-eez

---

## E

| | |
|---|---|
| Ebed-Melech ---- | EE-behd-MEE-lehk |
| Ebenezer -------- | eh-behn-EE-zer |
| Ecbatana --------- | ehk-BAT-uh-nuh |
| Ecclesiastes ------ | eh-klee-sih-AS-teez |
| Eden ------------ | EE-d'n |
| Edom ------------ | EE-duhm |
| Egypt ------------ | EE-dzhihpt |
| Egyptians --------- | ee-DZHIHP-shuhnz |
| Elamites --------- | EE-luh-maits |
| Eldad ------------ | EHL-dad |
| Eleazar ----------- | ehl-ee-AY-zer |
| Electrum -------- | ee-LEHK-truhm |
| Eli --------------- | EE-lai |
| Eli, Eli, lema ------ | AY-lee, AY-lee, luh-MAH |
| sabachthani ---- | sah-bahk-TAH-nee |
| Eliab ------------- | ee-LAI-ab |
| Eliakim ----------- | ee-LAI-uh-kihm |
| Eliezer ----------- | ehl-ih-EE-zer |
| Elihu ------------ | ee-LAI-hyoo |
| Elijah ------------ | ee-LAI-dzhuh |
| Elim ------------- | EE-lihm |
| Elimelech --------- | ee-LIHM-eh-lehk |
| Elisha ------------ | ee-LAI-shuh |

| | |
|---|---|
| Eliud ------------ | ee-LAI-uhd |
| Elizabeth -------- | ee-LIHZ-uh-b'th |
| Elkanah ---------- | ehl-KAY-nuh |
| Elnathan --------- | ehl-NAY-th'n |
| Eloi, Eloi, -------- | AY-lo-ee, AY-lo-ee, |
| lema ----------- | luh-MAH |
| sabachthani ---- | sah-bahk-TAH-nee |
| Elymais ---------- | ehl-ih-MAY-ihs |
| Emiliani --------- | ay-mee-lee-AH-nee |
| Emmanuel ------- | eh-MAN-yoo-ehl |
| Emmaus --------- | eh-MAY-uhs |
| Enmity ---------- | EHN-mih-tee |
| Epaenetus-------- | ee-PEE-nee-tuhs |
| Epaphras -------- | EH-puh-fras |
| Epaphroditus ---- | ee-paf-ro-DAI-tuhs |
| Epah------------- | EE-puh |
| Ephah ----------- | EE-fuh |
| Ephesians -------- | eh-FEE-zhuhnz |
| Ephesus ---------- | EH-fuh-suhs |
| Ephphatha ------- | EHF-uh-thuh |
| Ephphathy ------- | EHF-uh-thee |
| Ephraim --------- | EE-fray-ihm |
| Ephraimite ------- | EE-fray-ihm-ait |
| Ephratha --------- | EHF-ruh-thuh |
| Ephrathah ------- | EHF-ruh-thuh |
| Ephrem (deacon)-- | EHF-rehm |
| Ephron ---------- | EE-frawn |

| | |
|---|---|
| Epiphanes | eh-PIHF-uh-neez |
| Erastus | ee-RAS-tuhs |
| Esau | EE-saw |
| Espoused | eh-SPAUZD |
| Esther | EHS-ter |
| Ethanim | EHTH-uh-nihm |
| Ethiopia | ee-thee-O-pee-uh |
| Ethiopian | ee-thee-O-pee-uhn |
| Eunuch | YOO-nuhk |
| Euphrates | yoo-FRAY-teez |
| Eusebius | yoo-SEE-bee-uhs |
| Evangelist | ee-VAN-dzhuh-lihst |
| Exhorting | ehg-ZORT-ihng |
| Exodus | EHK-so-duhs |
| Exorcised | EHK-sawr-saizd |
| Expiate | EHKS-pee-ayt |
| Expiated | EHKS-pee-ayt-ehd |
| Expiation | ehks-pee-AY-shuhn |
| Exultantly | ehg-ZUHL-tent-lee |
| Ezekiel | eh-ZEE-kee-'l |
| Ezra | EHZ-ruh |

---

### F

| | |
|---|---|
| Fabian | FAY-bih-uhn |
| Felicity | feh-LIHS-ih-tee |
| Felix | FEE-lihks |

| | |
|---|---|
| Festus | FEHS-*too*s |
| Fidelis of | fih-DAY-lihs uhv |
| Sigmaringen | sihg-muh-RIHNG-ehn |
| Frankincense | FRANGK-ihn-sehns |

## G

| | |
|---|---|
| Gabbatha | GAB-uh-thuh |
| Gabriel | GAY-bree-'l |
| Gadarene | GAD-uh-reen |
| Gaius | GAY-yuhs |
| Galatan | GAL-uh-tuhn |
| Galatia | guh-LAY-shih-uh |
| Galilean | gal-ih-LEE-uhn |
| Galileans | gal-ih-LEE-uhnz |
| Galilee | GAL-ih-lee |
| Gallio | GAL-ih-o |
| Gamaliel | guh-MAY-lih-ehl |
| Gaza | GAH-zuh |
| Gehazi | gee-HAY-zai |
| Gehenna | geh-HEHN-uh |
| Genealogy | dzhee-nee-AH-lo-dzhee |
| Genesis | DZHEHN-uh-sihs |
| Gennesaret | gehn-NEHS-uh-reht |
| Gentile | DZHEHN-tail |
| Gentiles | DZHEHN-tailz |

| | |
|---|---|
| Gera | DZHEE-ruh |
| Gerasenes | DZHEHR-uh-seenz |
| Gerizim | dzheh-RAI-zihm |
| Gethsemane | gehth-SEHM-uh-nee |
| Gibeon | GIHB-ee-uhn |
| Gideon | GIHD-ee-uhn |
| Gilead | GIHL-ee-uhd |
| Gilgal | GIHL-gal |
| Girgashites | GER-guh-shaits |
| God | GAHD (not GAWD) |
| Golgotha | GAHL-guh-thuh |
| Goliath | go-LAI-uhth |
| Gomorrah | guh-MAWR-uh |
| Gonzaga | guhn-ZAH-guh |
| Goshen | GO-shuhn |
| Gozan | GO-zan |

## H

| | |
|---|---|
| Habakkuk | huh-BAK-uhk |
| Habor | HAY-bawr |
| Hadadrimmon | hay-dad-RIHM-uhn |
| Hades | HAY-deez |
| Haggai | HAG-ay-ai |
| Hagur | HAH-goor |
| Halah | HAY-luh |
| Haman | HAY-muhn |

| | |
|---|---|
| Hananiah | han-uh-NAI-uh |
| Hannah | HAN-uh |
| Haran | HAY-ruhn |
| Hazael | HAZ-ay-ehl |
| Hebrews | HEE-brooz |
| Hebron | HEE-bruhn |
| Heedfully | HEED-fool-ee |
| Heifer | HEH-fer |
| Hellenists | HEHL-uhn-ihsts |
| Hemorrhages | HEHM-uh-rihdzh'z |
| Hermes | HER-meez |
| Herod | HEHR-uhd |
| Herodians | hehr-O-dee-uhnz |
| Herodias | hehr-O-dee-uhs |
| Hezekiah | heh-zeh-KAI-uh |
| Hezikiah | heh-zih-KAI-uh |
| Hezron | HEHZ-ruhn |
| Hilary | HIHL-uh-ree |
| Hilkiah | hihl-KAI-uh |
| Hippolytus | hih-PAHL-ih-tuhs |
| Hireling | HAI-er-lihng |
| Hittite | HIH-tait |
| Hivite | HAI-vait |
| Holocaust | HAHL-o-kawst |
| Holocausts | HAHL-o-kawsts |
| Homage | HAH-muhdzh |
| | (not AH-muhdzh) |

| | |
|---|---|
| Hophni | HAHF-nai |
| Horeb | HAWR-ehb |
| Hosanna | ho-ZAH-nuh |
| Hosea | ho-ZEE-uh |
| Hoshea | ho-SHEE-uh |
| Hur | HER |
| Hymns | HIHMZ |
| Hypocrites | HIHP-uh-krihts |
| Hyssop | HIH-suhp |

## I

| | |
|---|---|
| Iconium | ai-KO-nih-uhm |
| Iddo | IHD-o |
| Idumea | ih-dzhoo-MEE-uh |
| Ignatius | ihg-NAY-shuhs |
| Immorality | ih-mor-RAL-ih-tee |
| Immortality | ih-mor-TAL-ih-tee |
| Irenaeus | ai-rehn-EE-uhs |
| Irreproachable | eer-ih-PROTSH-uh-b'l |
| Isaac | AI-zuhk |
| Isaiah | ai-ZAY-uh |
| Iscariot | ihs-KEHR-ee-uht |
| Ishmael | ISH-may-ehl |
| Ishmaelites | ISH-may-ehl-aits |
| Isles | AILZ |
| Israel | IHZ-ray-ehl |

| | |
|---|---|
| Israelite ----------- | IHZ-rih-ehl-ait |
| Israelites ---------- | IHZ-rih-ehl-aits |
| Italica ------------ | ih-TAL-ih-kuh |
| Ituraea ------------ | ih-TSHOOR-ree-uh |

---

## J

| | |
|---|---|
| Jaar --------------- | DZHAY-ahr |
| Jabbok ------------ | DZHAB-uhk |
| Jacob ------------- | DZHAY-kuhb |
| Jairus ------------- | DZHAI-roos |
| Januarius ---------- | dzhan-yoo-EHR-ee-uhs |
| Javan -------------- | DZHAY-van |
| Jebusites ---------- | DZHEHB-oo-zaits |
| Jechoniah --------- | dzhehk-o-NAI-uh |
| Jeconiah ---------- | dzhehk-o-NAI-uh |
| Jehoash ----------- | dzhee-HO-ash |
| Jehoiachim ------- | dzhee-HOI-uh-kihm |
| Jehoiachin ------- | dzhee-HOI-uh-kihn |
| Jehoiada ---------- | dzhee-HOI-uh-duh |
| Jehoram ---------- | dzhee-HOR-am |
| Jehoshaphat ------ | dzhee-HAHSH-uh-fat |
| Jehosheba --------- | dzhee-HAHSH-ee-buh |
| Jehozadak --------- | dzhee-HOZ-uh-dak |
| Jehu -------------- | DZHEE-hyoo |
| Jemimah ---------- | dzhee-MAI-muh |
| Jephthah ---------- | DZHEHF-thuh |

| | |
|---|---|
| Jeremiah | dzhehr-eh-MAI-uh |
| Jericho | DZHEHR-ih-ko |
| Jeroboam | dzhehr-o-BO-uhm |
| Jeroham | dzhee-RO-ham |
| Jerusalem | dzheh-ROO-suh-lehm |
| Jesreel | DZHEHZ-reel |
| Jesse | DZHEH-see |
| Jesus | DZHEE-zuhs |
| Jethro | DZHEHTH-ro |
| Jezreelite | DZHEHZ-ree-ehl-ait |
| Joab | DZHO-ab |
| Joachim | DZHO-uh-kihm |
| Joanna | dzho-AN-uh |
| Joash | DZHO-ash |
| Job | DZHOB |
| Joel | DZHO-ehl |
| Jogues | DZHOGZ |
| John | DZHAHN |
| Jonah | DZHO-nuh |
| Jonathan | DZHAHN-uh-th'n |
| Joppa | DZHAH-puh |
| Joram | DZHO-ram |
| Jordan | DZHAWR-d'n |
| Josaphat | DZHAH-suh-fat |
| Joseph | DZHO-z'f |
| Joses | DZHO-seez |
| Joshua | DZHAH-shoo-uh |

| | |
|---|---|
| Josiah | dzho-SAI-uh |
| Jotham | DZHO-thuhm |
| Judah | DZHOO-duh |
| Judaism | DZHOO-duh-ihz'm |
| Judas | DZHOO-duhs |
| Judas Iscariot | DZHOO-duhs ihs-KEHR-ee-uht |
| Judea | dzhoo-DEE-uh |
| Judean | dzhoo-DEE-uhn |
| Junias | DZHOO-nih-uhs |
| Justin | DZHUHS-tihn |
| Justus | DZHUHS-tuhs |

## K

| | |
|---|---|
| Kadesh | KAY-dehsh |
| Kanty | KAN-tee |
| Kedesh | KEE-dehsh |
| Keren-Happuch | KEHR-ehn-HAP-*ook* |
| Keziah | keh-ZAI-uh |
| Kidron | KIHD-ruhn |
| Kiriatharba | kihr-ee-ath-AHR-buh |
| Kish | KIHSH |
| Korban | KAWR-bahn |
| Kors | KORZ |

## L

| | |
|---|---|
| Laban | LAY-b'n |
| Lairs | LEHRZ |
| Lamentations | lam-ehn-TAY-shuhnz |
| Laodicea | lay-o-dih-SEE-uh |
| Laodiceans | lay-o-dih-SEE-uhnz |
| Lateran | LAT-er-uhn |
| Laud | LAWD |
| Lazarus | LAZ-er-uhs |
| Leah | LEE-uh |
| Leavened | LEHV-uhnd |
| Lebanon | LEH-buh-nuhn |
| Leonardi | lee-aw-NAR-dee |
| Leprosy | LEHP-ruh-see |
| Leprous | LEHP-ruhs |
| Levi | LEE-vai |
| Levites | LEE-vaits |
| Levitical | leh-VIH-tih-k'l |
| Leviticus | leh-VIH-tih-k*oo*s |
| Libya | LIH-bih-uh |
| Licentiousness | lai-SEHN-shuhs-nihs |
| Liguori | lih-G**OO**-ree |
| Lima, Rose of | LEE-muh, roz uhv |
| Lineage | LIHN-ee-ihdzh |
| Lintel | LIHN-tuhl |
| Loincloths | LOIN-klaw*thz* |

| | |
|---|---|
| Lourdes ----------- | LOORD |
| Lucius ------------ | LOO-shih-uhs |
| Lud -------------- | LUHD |
| Luke ------------- | LOOK |
| Luminaries ------- | LOO-mihn-ehr-eez |
| Luz -------------- | LUHZ |
| Lwanga ----------- | luh-WAHNG-guh |
| Lycaonian -------- | lihk-ay-O-nih-uhn |
| Lydda ------------ | LIH-duh |
| Lydia ------------ | LIH-dih-uh |
| Lyres ------------ | LAI-erz |
| Lysanias ---------- | lai-SAY-nih-uhs |
| Lysias ------------ | LIH-sih-uhs |
| Lystra ------------ | LIHS-truh |

## M

| | |
|---|---|
| Maccabees -------- | MAK-uh-beez |
| Macedon --------- | MAS-uh-duhn |
| Macedonia ------- | mas-eh-DO-nih-uh |
| Machir ----------- | MAY-kihr |
| Machpelah -------- | mak-PEE-luh |
| Magdala ---------- | MAG-duh-luh |
| Magdalene ------- | MAG-duh-lehn |
| Magi ------------- | MAY-dzhai |
| Mahlon ----------- | MAH-luhn |
| Malachi ----------- | MAL-uh-kai |

| | |
|---|---|
| Malchiah | mal-KAI-uh |
| Malchus | MAL-kuhs |
| Mammon | MAM-uhn |
| Mamre | MAM-ree |
| Manaen | MAN-uh-ehn |
| Manasseh | man-AS-eh |
| Mankind | man-KAIND |
| Manna | MAN-uh |
| Manoah | muh-NO-uh |
| Marcellinus | mahr-suh-LAI-nuhs |
| Mark | MAHRK |
| Marrow | MEHR-o |
| Martin de Porres | MAHR-tihn deh PAWR-ehz |
| Mary | MEHR-ee |
| Massah | MAH-suh |
| Mattan | MAT-uhn |
| Mattaniah | mat-uh-NAI-uh |
| Mattathias | mat-uh-THAI-uhs |
| Matthan | MAT-than |
| Matthew | MATH-yoo |
| Matthias | muh-THAI-uhs |
| Medad | MEE-dad |
| Medes | MEEDZ |
| Media | MEE-dih-uh |
| Megiddo | mee-GIH-do |
| Meholah | mee-HO-luh |

| | |
|---|---|
| Melchizedek ----- | mehl-KIHZ-eh-dehk |
| Mene ------------ | MEE-nee |
| Meribah --------- | MEHR-ih-bah |
| Meshach --------- | MEE-shak |
| Mesopotamia ---- | mehs-uh-po-TAY-mih-uh |
| Messiah ---------- | meh-SAI-uh |
| Methodius ------- | meh-THO-dee-uhs |
| Micah ----------- | MAI-kuh |
| Micaiah ---------- | mai-KAY-yuh |
| Midian ----------- | MIH-dih-uhn |
| Midianite -------- | MIH-dih-uhn-ait |
| Miki ------------- | MEE-kee |
| Milcom ---------- | MIHL-kahm |
| Miletus ---------- | mai-LEE-tuhs |
| Minions --------- | MIHN-yuhnz |
| Minnith --------- | MIHN-ihth |
| Mire ------------- | MAI-er |
| Miriam ---------- | MIHR-ih-uhm |
| Mishael ---------- | MIHSH-uh-ehl |
| Mitre ------------ | MAI-ter |
| Mizpah ---------- | MIHZ-puh |
| Moab ------------ | MO-ab |
| Moabite --------- | MO-ab-ait |
| Moabitess -------- | MO-ah-bai-tihs |
| Modein ---------- | MO-deen |
| Molech ---------- | MO-lehk |

| | |
|---|---|
| Mordecai | MAWR-deh-kai |
| Moreh | MO-reh |
| Moriah | maw-RAI-uh |
| Mosaic | mo-ZAY-ihk |
| Mosoch | MAH-sahk |
| Myriad | MIHR-ih-uhd |
| Myrrh | MER |
| Mysia | MIH-shih-uh |

## N

| | |
|---|---|
| Naaman | NAY-uh-muhn |
| Naboth | NAY-buhth |
| Nahor | NAY-hawr |
| Nahshon | NAH-shuhn |
| Nahum | NAY-huhm |
| Naim | NAY-ihm |
| Nain | NAY-ihn |
| Naomi | NAY-o-mee |
| Naphtali | NAF-tuh-lai |
| Nathan | NAY-thuhn |
| Nathanael | nuh-THAN-ay-ehl |
| Nazarene | naz-uh-REEN |
| Nazareth | NAZ-uh-rehth |
| Nazirite | NAZ-uh-rait |
| Nazorean | naz-aw-REE-uhn |
| Neapolis | nee-AP-o-lihs |

| | |
|---|---|
| Nebat ----------- | NEE-bat |
| Nebo ------------ | NAY-bo (name of God); NEE-bo (place) |
| Nebuchadnezzar -- | neh-byoo-kuhd-NEHZ-er |
| Nebuzaradan ----- | neh-byoo-zahr-AY-dan |
| Negeb ----------- | NEH-gehb |
| Nehemiah -------- | nee-hee-MAI-uh |
| Nehushta -------- | nee-HUHSH-tuh |
| Nephtali --------- | NEHF-tih-lee |
| Ner -------------- | NER |
| Nereus ---------- | NEE-roos |
| Neri ------------- | NEE-rai |
| Nether ---------- | NEH*TH*-er |
| Netherworld ----- | NEH*TH*-er-werld |
| Nicanor --------- | nai-KAY-nawr |
| Nicodemus ------ | nih-ko-DEE-muhs |
| Nicolaus --------- | nih-ko-LAY-uhs |
| Niger ------------ | NAI-dzher |
| Nimshi ---------- | NIHM-shai |
| Nineveh --------- | NIHN-eh-veh |
| Ninevites -------- | NIHN-eh-vaits |
| Nisan ----------- | NAI-san |
| Noah ------------ | NO-uh |
| Nun ------------- | NUHN |

## O

| | |
|---|---|
| Obed ------------ | O-behd |
| Obed-Edom ----- | O-behd-EE-duhm |
| Og -------------- | AHG |
| Olivet ----------- | AH-lih-veht |
| Omega ----------- | o-MAY-guh |
| Onesimus -------- | o-NEH-sih-muhs |
| Ophir ----------- | O-fer |
| Ophrah ---------- | OF-ruh |
| Orion ----------- | aw-RAI-uhn |
| Orpah ----------- | AWR-pah |

## P

| | |
|---|---|
| Padua ------------ | PAD-dzhoo-uh |
| Pamphylia ------- | pam-FIHL-ih-uh |
| Pancras ---------- | PAN-kras |
| Paola ------------ | pah-O-luh |
| Paphos ----------- | PAY-fuhs |
| Papyrus ---------- | puh-PAI-ruhs |
| Parable ---------- | PEHR-uh-buhl |
| Parables ---------- | PEHR-uh-buhlz |
| Paraclete --------- | PEHR-uh-kleet |
| Paran ------------ | PAY-ran |
| Parapet ---------- | PEHR-uh-peht |
| Parath ----------- | PAH-rath |
| Parmenas -------- | PAHR-mee-nas |

| | |
|---|---|
| Parthians | PAHR-thee-uhnz |
| Pasch | PASK |
| Paschal | PAS-k'l |
| Passover | PAS-o-ver |
| Patmos | PAT-mos |
| Patriarch | PAY-trih-ahrk |
| Patriarchs | PAY-trih-ahrks |
| Paucinus | paw-SAI-nuhs |
| Pekah | PEE-kah |
| Penninah | pee-NIHN-uh |
| Pentecost | PEHN-tee-kawst |
| Penuel | pee-NYOO-ehl |
| Peres | PEE-rehs |
| Perez | PEE-rehz |
| Perga | PER-guh |
| Perizzites | PEHR-ih-zaits |
| Perpetua | per-PEH-tshoo-uh |
| Persia | PER-zhuh |
| Persians | PER-zhuhnz |
| Peter Chanel | PEE-ter shuh-NEHL |
| Phanuel | FAN-yoo-ehl |
| Pharan | FAHR-ahn |
| Pharaoh | FEHR-o |
| Pharisee | FEHR-ih-see |
| Pharisees | FEHR-ih-seez |
| Pharpar | FAHR-pahr |
| Philemon | fih-LEE-muhn |

| | |
|---|---|
| Philippi ----------- | fih-LIHP-ai |
| Philippians -------- | fih-LIHP-ih-uhnz |
| Philistia ----------- | fih-LIHS-tih-uh |
| Philistines --------- | FEE-lihs-tihnz |
| Phinehas ----------- | FIHN-ee-uhs |
| Phoenicia --------- | fee-NIHSH-ih-uh |
| Phogor ----------- | FO-gawr |
| Phrygia ----------- | FRIH-dzhih-uh |
| Phylacteries ------- | fih-LAK-ter-eez |
| Pi-Hahiroth ------ | pai-huh-HAI-rahth |
| Pilate ------------- | PAI-luht |
| Pisgah ----------- | PIHZ-guh |
| Pisidia ----------- | pih-SIH-dih-uh |
| Pithom ----------- | PAI-thahm |
| Pleiades ----------- | PLEE-uh-deez |
| Polycarp ---------- | PAH-lee-kahrp |
| Pomegranates ---- | PAHM-gran-ihts |
| Pontian ----------- | PAHN-shuhn |
| Pontius Pilate ---- | PAHN-sh*oo*s PAI-luht |
| Pontus ----------- | PAHN-tuhs |
| Portico ----------- | PAWR-tih-ko |
| Portugal ---------- | PAWR-tshuh-guhl |
| Praetorium ------- | pray-TAWR-ih-uhm |
| Predetermined --- | pree-dee-TER-mihnd |
| Presbyter --------- | PREHZ-bih-ter |
| Principality ------- | prihn-sih-PAL-uh-tee |
| Principalities ----- | prihn-sih-PAL-uh-teez |

| | |
|---|---|
| Prisca ------------ | PRIHS-kuh |
| Prochorus -------- | PRAH-kaw-ruhs |
| Procurator ------- | PRAH-kyoor-ay-ter |
| Procuring -------- | pro-KYOOR-ihng |
| Prodigies -------- | PRAH-dih-dzheez |
| Profaned --------- | pro-FAYND |
| Prophesied ------- | PRAH-feh-said |
| Prophesy (verb) -- | PRAH-feh-sai |
| Prophetess ------- | PRAH-feh-tehs |
| Prostrate -------- | PRAHS-trayt |
| Prostrated -------- | PRAHS-trayt-ehd |
| Psalms ------------ | SAHMZ |
| Publius ----------- | PUHB-lih-uhs |
| Purification ------ | pyoor-ih-fih-KAY-shuhn |
| Put --------------- | PUHT |
| Puteoli ----------- | pyoo-TEE-o-lai |

## Q

| | |
|---|---|
| Qoheleth -------- | ko-HEHL-ehth |
| Quartus ----------- | KWAR-tuhs |
| Quirinius -------- | kwai-RIHN-ih-uhs |

## R

| | |
|---|---|
| Raamses ---------- | ray-AM-seez |
| Rabbah ----------- | RAB-uh |

| | |
|---|---|
| Rabbi ------------ | RAB-ai |
| Rabboni ---------- | ra-BO-nai |
| Raga ------------ | RAH-guh |
| Raguel ----------- | rah-GYOO-ehl |
| Rahab ----------- | RAY-hab |
| Ram ------------- | RAM |
| Ramah ---------- | RAY-muh |
| Ramathaim ------ | ray-muh-THAY-ihm |
| Rapael ----------- | RAY-pay-ehl |
| Raphael ---------- | RAY-fay-ehl |
| Rebekah---------- | ree-BEHK-uh |
| Recompense ----- | REH-kuhm-pehns |
| Reconciliation --- | reh-kuhn-sih-lee-AY-shuhn |
| Redemption ----- | ree-DEHM-shuhn |
| Refulgence ------ | ree-FOOL-dzhents |
| Rehoboam ------ | ree-ho-BO-am |
| Remaliah -------- | rehm-uh-LAI-uh |
| Rephidim -------- | REHF-ih-dihm |
| Responsorial----- | ree-spahn-SAWR-ee-uhl |
| Reuben ---------- | ROO-b'n |
| Revelation ------- | reh-veh-LAY-shuhn |
| Rezin ------------ | REE-zihn |
| Rhegium -------- | REE-dzhee-uhm |
| Riblah ----------- | RIHB-luh |
| Righteous ------- | RAI-tshuhs |

| | |
|---|---|
| Righteousness --- | RAI-tshuhs-nehs |
| Ritual ----------- | RIH-tshoo-*ool* |
| Romuald -------- | RO-moo-ahld |
| Rue (noun) ------ | ROO |
| Rufus----------- | ROO-fuhs |

---

## S

| | |
|---|---|
| Sabbath ---------- | SAB-uhth |
| Sabeans ---------- | suh-BEE-uhnz |
| Sadducees ------- | SAD-dzhoo-seez |
| Salamis ---------- | SAL-uh-mihs |
| Salem ----------- | SAY-lehm |
| Salishah ---------- | suh-LEE-shuh |
| Salmon ---------- | SAL-muhn |
| Salome ---------- | suh-LO-mee |
| Salu ------------ | SAYL-yoo |
| Samaria ---------- | suh-MEHR-ih-uh |
| Samaritan -------- | suh-MEHR-ih-tuhn |
| Samothrace ------ | SAM-o-thrays |
| Samson ---------- | SAM-s'n |
| Samuel ---------- | SAM-yoo-uhl |
| Sanctification ---- | sang-tih-fih-KAY-shuhn |
| Sanctify ---------- | SANG-tih-fai |
| Sanctuary -------- | SANG-tshoo-ehr-ee |
| Sanhedrin ------- | san-HEE-drihn |
| Sapphires -------- | SAF-fai-erz |

| | |
|---|---|
| Sarah | SEHR-uh |
| Sarai | SAY-rai |
| Saraph | SAY-raf |
| Sardis | SAHR-dihs |
| Saul | SAWL |
| Savior | SAYV-yer |
| Scepter | SEHP-ter |
| Scholastica | skuh-LAS-tih-kuh |
| Scimitar | SIHM-ih-ter |
| Scythian | SIH-thee-uhn |
| Seah | SEE-uh |
| Seba | SEE-buh |
| Seir | SEE-er |
| Seleucia | seh-LOO-shih-uh |
| Sennacherib | seh-NAK-er-ihb |
| Seraphim | SEHR-uh-fihm |
| Seth | SEHTH |
| Shaalim | SHAY-uh-lihm |
| Shadrach | SHAY-drak |
| Shalmaneser | shal-muh-NEE-zer |
| Shalom | shuh-LOM |
| Shammah | SHAM-uh |
| Shaphan | SHAY-fuhn |
| Shaphat | SHAY-fat |
| Sharon | SHEHR-uhn |
| Shealtiel | shee-AL-tih-ehl |

| | |
|---|---|
| Shear-Jashub ----- | SHEE-ahr-DZHAH-shuhb |
| Sheba ------------ | SHEE-buh |
| Shebna ----------- | SHEHB-nuh |
| Shechem --------- | SHEE-kehm |
| Shekel ----------- | SHEHK-uhl |
| Shiloh ----------- | SHAI-lo |
| Shilonite --------- | SHAI-lo-nait |
| Shimei ----------- | SHIHM-ee-ai |
| Shinar ----------- | SHAI-nahr |
| Shunammite ----- | SHOO-nam-ait |
| Shunem --------- | SHOO-nehm |
| Shur ------------- | SHOOR |
| Sidon ------------ | SAI-duhn |
| Sidonians -------- | sai-DO-nee-uhnz |
| Siena ------------ | see-EHN-uh |
| Siesta ------------ | see-EHS-tuh |
| Sieve ------------ | SIHV |
| Sihon ------------ | SAI-hon |
| Silas ------------- | SAI-luhs |
| Siloam ----------- | sih-LO-uhm |
| Silvanus ---------- | sihl-VAY-nuhs |
| Simeon ----------- | SIHM-ee-uhn |
| Simon ----------- | SAI-muhn |
| Simon of Cyrene-- | SAI-muhn uhv sai-REE-nee |
| Sin (desert) ------ | SIHN |

| | |
|---|---|
| Sinai | SAI-nai |
| Sinews | SIHN-yooz |
| Sirach | SAI-rak |
| Sistrum | SIHS-truhm |
| Sixtus | SIKS-tuhs |
| Smitten | SMIHT'n |
| Smyrna | SMER-nuh |
| Sodom | SAH-duhm |
| Sojourn | SO-dzhern |
| Sojourning | SO-dzhern-ihng |
| Solicitude | so-LIHS-ih-tyood |
| Solomon | SAH-luh-muhn |
| Sosthenes | SAHS-thee-neez |
| Sovereignty | SAH-vrehn-tee |
| Spikenard | SPAIK-nahrd |
| Stachys | STAY-kihs |
| Stanislaus | STAN-ihs-laws |
| Stephen | STEE-v'n |
| Stewardship | STOO-erd-shihp |
| Sublimity | suhb-LIHM-ih-tee |
| Succoth | SUHK-ahth |
| Supplications | suhp-lih-KAY-shuhnz |
| Swaddling | SWAHD-lihng |
| Sychar | SAI-ker |
| Syene | sai-EE-nee |
| Symeon | SIHM-ee-uhn |
| Synagogue | SIHN-uh-gahg |

| | |
|---|---|
| Synagogues ------ | SIHN-uh-gahgz |
| Syria ------------ | SIHR-ee-uh |
| Syrian ----------- | SIHR-ee-uhn |
| Syro-Phoenician -- | SIHR-o-fee-NIHSH-ih-uhn |

---

## T

| | |
|---|---|
| Tabeel ----------- | TAY-bee-ehl |
| Tabitha ---------- | TAB-ih-thuh |
| Talitha Koum ---- | TAL-ih-thuh KOOM |
| Tamar ----------- | TAY-mer |
| Tarshish --------- | TAHR-shihsh |
| Tarsus ----------- | TAHR-suhs |
| Tekel ------------ | TEH-keel |
| Terah ------------ | TEE-ruh |
| Terebinth -------- | TEHR-ee-bihnth |
| Tertius ----------- | TER-shih-uhs |
| Tethered --------- | TEH*TH*-erd |
| Tetrarch --------- | TEH-trahrk |
| Thaddeus -------- | THAD-dee-uhs |
| Theophilus ------ | thee-AH-fih-luhs |
| Theresa ---------- | ter-EE-suh |
| Thessalonians ---- | theh-suh-LO-nih-uhnz |
| Thessalonica ----- | theh-suh-LAHN-ih-kuh |
| Thisbe ----------- | THIHZ-bee |
| Thyatira --------- | thai-uh-TAI-ruh |

| | |
|---|---|
| Tiberius | tai-BIHR-ih-uhs |
| Timaeus | tai-MEE-uhs |
| Timbrel | TIHM-br'l |
| Timon | TAI-muhn |
| Timothy | TIH-muh-thee |
| Tishbe | TIHSH-bee |
| Tishbite | TIHSH-bait |
| Tithe | TAI*TH* |
| Titus | TAI-tuhs |
| Titus Justus | TAI-tuhs DZHUHS-tuhs |
| Tobiah | to-BAI-uh |
| Tobit | TO-biht |
| Tohu | TO-hyoo |
| Tours | T*OO*R |
| Trachonitis | trak-o-NAI-tihs |
| Transfigured | trans-FIHG-yerd |
| Transgression | trans-GREHSH-uhn |
| Tribulation | trihb-yoo-LAY-shuhn |
| Tribunal | trai-BYOO-nuhl |
| Troas | TRO-ahs |
| Tubal | TYOO-b'l |
| Turibius de Mongrovejo | tuh-RIHB-ee-uhs day mahn-gro-VAY-ho |
| Tychicus | TIH-kih-kuhs |
| Tyre | TAI-er |
| Tyrian | TIHR-ih-uhn |

## U

| | |
|---|---|
| Uncircumcision -- | uhn-ser-kuhm-SIHZH-uhn |
| Unleavened ------ | uhn-LEHV-uhnd |
| Ur ------------- | ER |
| Urbanus --------- | er-BAY-nuhs |
| Uriah ----------- | yoo-RAI-uh |
| Uzziah ---------- | yoo-ZAI-uh |

## V

| | |
|---|---|
| Vainglory -------- | VAYN-glaw-ree |
| Vercelli ---------- | ver-TSHEHL-ee |
| Vesture ---------- | vehs-TSHOOR |
| Vianney --------- | vee-uh-NAY |
| Vindication ------ | vihn-dih-KAY-shuhn |
| Vintager --------- | VIHN-tih-dzher |

## W-X-Y

| | |
|---|---|
| Wadi ------------ | WAH-dee |
| Wadi Cherith ---- | WAH-dee KEE-rihth |
| Wenceslaus ------ | WEHN-sehs-laws |
| Xavier ----------- | ZAY-vee-er |
| Yahweh-Yireh --- | YAH-weh-yer-AY |
| Yahweh-Shalom - | YAH-weh-shuh-LOM |

## Z

| | |
|---|---|
| Zaccaria | zak-uh-RAI-uh |
| Zacchaeus | zak-KEE-uhs |
| Zadok | ZAY-dahk |
| Zarephath | ZEHR-ee-fath |
| Zarethan | ZEHR-ee-than |
| Zealot | ZEH-laht |
| Zebedee | ZEH-beh-dee |
| Zebulun | ZEH-byoo-luhn |
| Zechariah | zeh-kuh-RAI-uh |
| Zedekiah | zeh-dee-KAI-uh |
| Zephaniah | zeh-fuh-NAI-uh |
| Zerah | ZEE-ruh |
| Zeror | ZEE-rawr |
| Zerubbabel | zeh-RUH-buh-behl |
| Zeruiah | zeh-roo-AI-uh |
| Ziklag | ZIHK-lag |
| Zimri | ZIHM-rai |
| Zin | ZIHN |
| Zion | ZAI-uhn |
| Ziph | ZIHF |
| Zippor | ZIH-pawr |
| Zoar | ZO-er |
| Zorah | ZAWR-uh |
| Zuhf | ZUHF |
| Zuphite | ZUHF-ait |